Learn Portuguese

A Simple Guide to Learning Portuguese for Beginners, Including Grammar, Short Stories and Popular Phrases

Contents

Part 1: Portuguese

How to Learn Portuguese Fast, Including Grammar, Short Stories, and Useful Phrases

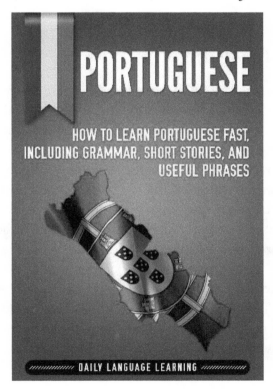

Introduction

Knowing more than one language is essential in many working environments. Globalization has made the world smaller, and thus, connecting to other people, sharing information and knowledge, while working together towards the same goal, has become inevitable. However, to do so successfully, the language barrier has to be overcome. Moreover, while it is true that English is the language more widely spoken across the globe, many other idioms are in high demand, and that may be very valuable in the near future, either for your personal or professional life. Portuguese is, without a doubt, one of them. Being the sixth most spoken language in the world, and the official language of Portugal, Brazil, Angola, Cape Verde, São Tomé and Príncipe, Guinea Bissau, Mozambique, Equatorial Guinea, and East Timor, Portuguese is, now more than ever, a skill very much worth having. This book aims to do just that—teach you the essentials of this new skill. At the very least, it is expected that *Portuguese: How to Learn Portuguese Fast, Including Grammar, Short Stories, and Useful Phrases* sets out the fundamentals of the language, allowing you to have the tools you need to carry on this path of knowledge.

When learning a language, you are learning so much more than a few words and grammar rules. You are subtly getting an insight into the thinking process involved in the creation of the language, the vast culture that encompasses a country, or several, the differences in customs and traditions, the expressions, and how they came about, and so much more. As you progress, you will find that the Portuguese language is complex and rich—just like its history and culture. So, if you feel discouraged at any point, think about how you're not only mastering a new skill, which takes time, but also, and more importantly, that you're getting to know a part of the world's history while enabling yourself to connect with others. How, you might ask? Because the role of the knowledge of a language is pivotal, as it allows people to bond with one another. It allows us to reach out, to share personal experiences and feelings, and to understand and be understood. Moreover, in a world in which everyone is struggling to acknowledge, accept and tolerate others, it is important that we start using language and words as the first and ultimate weapon. It is the supreme tool that enables every one of us to have a voice, be heard, and, much more importantly, to hear, listen, and understand—and, consequently, to empathize and connect. Besides, did you know that Portuguese derives from Latin? Because of that, Portuguese can be a great starting point to learn other Romance languages like French, Italian or Spanish. They share numerous words while many others are very similar; something you will definitely notice as soon as your vocabulary becomes richer.

So, the only thing left to do is wish you... ***Boa sorte!***

A Few Tips about Portuguese

The Portuguese Language has evolved throughout the years to adapt to its organic changes, current ways of speaking it and also to unite and unify it throughout the different Portuguese speaking countries. The Orthographic Agreement of 1990 has changed the spelling of many words and made the written PT Portuguese much more similar to the spoken BR Portuguese. Even though the agreement is from 1990, it was only applied in Portugal in 2010. However, there is some controversy when it comes to the use of this agreement; thus, many authors, writers, journalists, and academics choose to write in agreement with the Portuguese prior to the 1990 Orthographic Agreement. That is also the choice made in this book. However, if we think there might be something you need to be aware of, we will let you know. Nevertheless, if after reading this book, you read a Portuguese book or newspaper in which some words are spelled slightly different from what you have learned, don't worry. Both versions are equally accepted socially.

So, you already know that Portuguese is spoken in many countries around the world. The language is fundamentally the same throughout those countries, but it is only natural that some words, the pronunciation, the accents, popular sayings, and things of this nature, differ. A Portuguese-speaking person will undoubtedly understand another, regardless of where they come from. Nevertheless, all countries have throughout their extension many different accents, obviously. Some of them may even be really hard to understand for natives, so don't get frustrated if you happen to meet a Portuguese-speaking native with a thick accent—just ask him or her to speak slower or to *falar mais devagar, por favor!* Granted, that for the ones who are just beginning to learn the language, it can be confusing and even counter-productive to be presented to multiple countries' Portuguese at the same time. With that in mind, the choice of this book was to follow the Portuguese from Portugal norms. That includes sayings, pronunciation, spelling, and wording. However, because Brazil is becoming a very important country in the political scene, besides being a very popular tourist destination, some of the differences between both languages will be approached and presented to the reader, so that it is easier to make the transition and adapt. Again, whichever "version" of Portuguese you speak will be understood worldwide, but it is better to be acquainted with specific Brazilian terms so that everything goes smoothly if you ever happen to visit Brazil or meet a Brazilian. The differences can be compared to US English and British English, so there's not much to worry about.

One thing, however, that is worthy of being mentioned is the very Portuguese practice of being formal, linguistically, to show respect. Whenever a person is talking to someone they don't know, or just don't know very well, someone older, someone higher up in a hierarchical position, or even in a work environment, with coworkers, instead of the "tu" = "you" being used, the word "você" = "you" is used. But it isn't quite that simple. Even though using "tu" might not be appropriate, actually using or saying the word "você" isn't either. It may seem confusing, but when you're approaching someone and have to talk formally, you just omit the word "você", and continue building the sentence as if it was there all along. Then, instead of the verb being in the first person singular, the verb is conjugated in the third person singular, but «você» is either omitted or replaced by the person's name or just «o senhor / a senhora» (sir / ma'am). Look at these examples:

- Did you deliver the documents, sir? – *(Você) <u>Entregou</u> os documentos?* or *O senhor entregou os documentos?*
- You're doing a great job, ma'am! – *(Você) <u>Está</u> a fazer um trabalho fantástico!* or *A senhora está a fazer um trabalho fantástico!*
- Do you want to come by for dinner? – *(Você) <u>Quer</u> vir cá jantar?*

If this was an informal conversation, it would go like this:

- Did you deliver the documents? – *Tu <u>entregaste</u> os documentos?* or *Entregaste os documentos?*
- You're doing a great job! – *Tu <u>estás</u> a fazer um trabalho fantástico!* or *Estás a fazer um trabalho fantástico!*
- Do you want to come by for dinner? – *Tu <u>queres</u> vir cá jantar?* or *Queres vir cá jantar?*

With Brazilians, however, in the informal speech, instead of the word "tu", the word "você" is used. The sentences would be constructed as the first set of examples given, but without the omitted "você", meaning "você" is actually said. In the formal speech, there is a tendency to use "o senhor/a senhora" = "sir/madam" and hiding the "você". It may be hard to perceive or identify these differences and knowing how to use what and when. But there is no reason to fret. Learning a language as rich and complex as Portuguese takes time and effort. And it is that same effort that will be taken into account by the Portuguese. They will love the fact that you're speaking their language and may even help you with some tips.

Regarding the organization of the book, it starts by presenting the alphabet and how to pronounce each letter. Moving on, you will find how a sentence is built in Portuguese—we will start by deconstructing it to then, hopefully, enable you to build it from scratch. We'll approach several elements of the Portuguese grammar, namely the ones we deem absolutely fundamental, and after that, you will find four short stories that will portray real-life situations, which will hopefully allow you to connect more organically to the Portuguese language by dealing with it in a more dynamic context. After the short stories, there is a chapter that contains varied basic sentences that you may use in case you're visiting any Portuguese speaking country. Right at the end of the book, you will find a few lists that may help you on several different occasions or in certain situations.

Throughout the book, there will also be some exercises to put your Portuguese abilities to the test. After each short story—which is translated into English to facilitate comprehension—there will be a small quiz to test a wide variety of subjects. Every quiz, test or question is solved, but try to complete everything without looking for the right answer. Equally important is to follow the order of the book, and to read everything through and through (except for the pocket dictionary—go there any time you need, especially in the beginning), not just bits, at least in the first reading or first couple of readings. An overall view or understanding will make everything sink in more easily, even if, at first, it seems to be somewhat confusing.

Lastly, a few final tips to help you:

- Speak to yourself in Portuguese whenever you can;
- Walk around the house naming objects in Portuguese;
- Connect words to images. The memory clues images trigger will definitely help you retain the knowledge of what you have been studying;
- Try to think in Portuguese;
- If you know someone who's also trying to learn Portuguese, talk and write to them always in Portuguese and correct each other.

And now, we're all set. Let's start!

Chapter 1 – First Things First

Alphabet

Vowels

When saying the vowels a, e, i, o, u, they should sound like this: "a", like the "a" in "car; the "e", like the "e" in "tell"; "i", like the "ee" in "seed"; "o", like the "o" in "door"; and finally "u", like the "u" in "super". However, as we have seen many times throughout this book, things are not quite so simple. At several other times, for several other words, the way you read these vowels will depend on the words and the combination of letters. In fact, the sound the vowels "a", "e" and "o" make vary a lot since they have four different types of pronunciation:

> a) Open pronunciation;
> b) Closed pronunciation;
> c) Reduced pronunciation;
> d) Nasal pronunciation.

Below you'll find how every vowel is pronounced in each different situation.

> ➤ <u>"a":</u>

a) Like the "a" in "cat". This sound sometimes happens in the stressed syllable of a word, or if it contains the diacritical mark " ´ ";

b) Used when the "a" is at the end of the word but can be in the stressed syllable or anywhere else in the word. It is the case of the first two letters "a" on the name "Mariana". It sounds similar to the "u" in "butter";

c) This happens when the "a" is at the end of a word. The sound is reduced or almost non-existent. Again, with the name "Mariana", the pronunciation, if written, would look something like "ma-rian", the last "a" being practically non-existent;

d) In the word "ananás", the first two vowels are followed by a nasal sound, which makes them sound like the "a" in "anthropologist". With the diacritical marks "^" or "~", this vowel will also sound nasal.

➢ **"e":**

a) Like the "e" in "pet", when it is in the accentuated syllable or if it has the acute accent " ´ ";

b) When an "e" is not at the end of the word but can be in the stressed syllable. The sound is something similar to the "a" in "answer";

c) When the "e" is at the end of the word or between two consonants in the non-stressed syllable. The sound is very reduced or almost non-existent;

d) It will sound like the "e" in "enthusiasm". The diacritical mark "^" will also make it sound nasal.

➢ **"i" and "u":**

These two vowels are pronounced only with an open pronunciation. In a few words, they can also sound reduced when they are in between two consonants in a non-stressed syllable.

➢ **"o":**

a) When it is in the accentuated syllable or if it contains an acute accent;

b) When the "o" is not at the end of the word but can be in the stressed syllable. The sound is something similar to the "ou" sound in "soul";

c) When the "o" is at the end of the word, in a non-stressed syllable, or just by itself, as a definite article. This makes the "o" sound like an "u" or "oo", like in the word "super";

d) Like in the case of "a" and "e", this type of pronunciation happens every time the vowel is followed by an "n" or "m" or contains the diacritical mark "^" or "~". In words like "ponte" (bridge), the vowel will come out pretty nasalized, and it will sound something like "on" in the word "among".

Consonants

➤ **"B"** – always sounds just like the "b" in the word base;

➤ **"C"** – when it is followed by either an "e" or an "i", it has a soft sound as in "center". Followed by either an "a", "o", or "u", it has a hard sound as in "car".

➤ **"D"** – sounds as it does in English;

➤ **"F"** – sounds as it does in English;

➤ **"G"** – when is followed by an "a", "o", or "u", it has a hard sound like the "g" in "gun". When it is followed by an "e" or "I", it sounds like the "s" in "leisure";

➤ **"H"** – always silent in Portuguese, as it is in the word "hour";

➤ **"J"** – always pronounced like the "s" in leisure, no matter which vowel follows it;

➤ **"L"** – at the beginning of a word and between vowels, it always sounds like the "l" in "late". At the end of the word, it sounds just like it does in English;

➤ **"M"** – at the beginning of a word and between vowels, it sounds like the "m" in the word "mom". At the end of a word, it has a sound similar to the "n" in the word "cent";

➤ **"N"** – makes the same sound as the English "n" does, before or between vowels;

- ➢ **"P"** – sounds the same as in English;
- ➢ **"Q"** – sounds the same as "k";
- ➢ **"R"** – at the beginning of a word and when doubled, it has a hard sound, which is not very common in English. It can be somewhat similar to a hard accent when saying the words "hell" or "hot". When at the end of a word, or before or after a vowel, it has a soft sound, as the "r" in "heart";

- ➢ **"S"** – has a soft sound as in "salt" when it is positioned at the beginning of a word no matter which vowel follows it, and also when it's doubled. Before a consonant, it sounds hard as the "sh" in the word "shoe". Between two vowels, it sounds like a "z";
- ➢ **"T"** – sounds the same as in English;
- ➢ **"V"** – sounds the same as in English;
- ➢ **"X"** – the letter "x" can make several sounds – "s", "ch", "z", "cs", and "ss". The most usual sound is the "ch" sound, which is always used when "x" is at the beginning of a word, and it sounds like the "sh" in the word "shoe". At the end of a word, it always sounds as "cs", like "x" in the word "next".
- ➢ **"Z"** – sounds the same as in English. However, when it is at the end of a word, it sounds like "sh", as in "shot".

Pronunciation

The pronunciation of the words is probably one of the hardest things to get right when learning a language. If you study enough, you will master the mechanics of a language—its grammar and vocabulary— but getting the accent and the correct pronunciation right is almost always a hassle. Some people have it naturally—a gift that makes them have an aptitude for pronouncing words in other languages just like natives. In the end, it doesn't matter if the pronunciation is native-like—if you're understood and pronounce words correctly, you're all set. However, to achieve that (and especially if you want to have that native accent), you have to understand how to pronounce every word, and what rule applies to each word, depending on digraphs, diphthongs, or diacritical marks particularities.

To make things harder, it's possible to create new sounds in Portuguese by combining two letters in pairs like "ss", "rr", "lh", "nh", and "ch"; when using accent signs over the vowels (á, é, ó, ú, ê, ô, ã, õ, à); and when using the cedilla under the c – "ç". Here is what you should do to more easily identify where the stress syllable is, so you know where to accentuate the tone.

➤ Check the word to see if there is an accent:

If you find a tilde (~), an acute accent (´), a grave stress (`) or a circumflex mark (^), the stress will be on that syllable. So, if you have the word "ananás" (pineapple), and you divide the word into syllables, "A-na-nás", the stress will fall on the last syllable because that is where the diacritical mark is. Therefore, we have the following pronunciation: "a-na-*nás*", the highlighted letters being the stress syllables.

- Co-ra-*ção* (heart);
- *Fá*-cil (easy);
- *Grá*-tis (free);
- Con-fu-*são* (confusion);
- So-*má*-li-a (somalia).

So, remember: the first thing you should do is to check for a stress mark like the ones described, and if the word has one of those, then it will be easy to know where the stress of the word should go and which syllable you should pronounce more.

➤ When the word does not have a diacritical mark, then the stress of the word generally goes into the penultimate (i.e., the one before the last) syllable:

This is the second most important rule because, in general, words that are not accentuated by a stress mark have their penultimate syllable accentuated instead. For instance, the word "caminho" (path/way), which is divided into three syllables, "ca-mi-nho", has its stress syllable in "mi". As you can see, the penultimate syllable is the one stressed since no diacritical mark tells us otherwise.

Check out some other examples:

- Co-*mi*-da (Food);
- A-ven-tu-*rei*-ro (Adventurous);
- Ca-sa-*men*-to (Marriage);
- Com-pa-*nhi*-a (Company).

From the examples above you can conclude that the length of the word is not important. Whether it has two, three, four or even more syllables, if it does not have a diacritical mark, it will generally have its stress in the penultimate syllable.

Nevertheless, and even though this rule is applied in most of the cases, there are, of course, some exceptions. Here are some of those:

➢ Word ending in "i", "l", "r", "z", "im", "um", "ins", "uns":

In those cases, instead of being in the penultimate syllable, the stress shifts to the final syllable:

- Pa-*pel* (paper);
- Co-*mer* (eat);
- Sen-*ti* (I felt);
- A-*tum* (tuna);
- Vo-*raz* (voracious);
- Pin-gu-*im* (penguin);
- Pin-gu-*ins* (penguins);
- Al-*guns* (some).

➢ The sound of "lh" pair:

When an "l" is paired with an "h", the sound of the "lh" pair is somewhat similar to the double "l" in the word "million". However, you need to make sure the tip of your tongue touches the internal part of the top of your front teeth as you're pronouncing the syllable that contains the "lh" pair.

➤ The sound of "nh" pair:

When an "n" is paired with an "nh", the sound of the "nh" pair is the same sound as that of the "ñ" in Spanish. Unfortunately, there is no equivalent in the English language from which we can draw comparisons.

➤ The sound of "ch" pair:

When a "c" is paired with a "ch", you get the pair "ch", which sounds the same way as the "sh" sound in English, just like in the word "she".

➤ The sound of vowels with accent marks:

In Portuguese, the sound of the vowels changes when accent marks are used. Four different kinds of accent marks can be used on top of the vowels: acute (á, é, í, ó, ú), circumflex (ê, ô), tilde (ã, õ), and grave accent (à).

- The acute accent makes the vowels have an open sound:
  - Já, like the "a" in the word "bar";
  - Raíz, like the pronunciation of the letter "e" in English;
  - Café, like the letter "e" in the word "bed";
  - Avó, like the word "oh";
  - Baú, like the second "u" in the word "kung-fu".
- The circumflex makes the vowels sound closed:
  - Você, like the sound of the beginning of the word "hence";
  - Avô, like the beginning of the word "oat".
- The tilde makes the vowels sound nasal:
  - Mão;
  - Limões;
  - Capitães.
- The grave accent is used to indicate the contraction of two words represented by one word in a sentence, rather than for creating a new sound; for instance, the feminine definite

article "a" (the) and the preposition "a" (to). They become one word, and the grave accent is used on it, so "a" + "a" = "à". In this case, the sound of the "a" does not change at all. It continues the same as the name of the letter "a" in the alphabet, as well as the "á" (with the acute accent), as mentioned above.

➤ **The sound of the "ç":**

When the cedilla is used under a "c", the hard sound before an "a" or an "o" changes to the soft sound, like the "s" in the word "some".

➤ **The sound of nasal diphthongs:**

A nasal sound is a sound you produce forcing the air out of your nose. That is what happens, or what should happen when you pronounce the letters "m" and "n" in Portuguese. If the word ends in a diphthong—two vowels that are read together to form a single sound—like "ão", "au", "ao", "õe", "oi", "ãe", "ai", "ou", "ei", "ui", the stress also shifts to the end. For instance, if you have a word like "Macau", the stress will be in the last syllable, because this word ends with a diphthong.

Singular and plural

In Portuguese, nouns and adjectives both have plural forms. So, the first thing to retain is that in Portuguese, an adjective, in relation to the noun, has to agree in gender—masculine or feminine—and in number—singular or plural. We will find out more about the gender of words later. For now, let's focus on the singular or plural.

➤ **Words ending in a vowel:**

As a general rule, with words that end with a vowel, all you need to add is an "s" at the end. However, it can't be that easy, can it? Obviously, there are some exceptions. You should, in this sense, make sure when you're applying the rule that you're not coming across an exception. We will check out some situations in which words ending in a vowel don't follow this rule soon. Here are some examples of the general rule being applied:

- Cama leve (light bed) = camas leves
- Menina bonita (pretty girl) = meninas bonitas
- Menino alto (tall boy) = meninos altos

➤ **Words ending in an "l":**

With words that end in either "al" or "ul", just cut the "l" off and add an "is" to the end of it. If the word ends in either an "el" or "ol", cut the "l" off and add an "is" to the word, just like the previous case, but also add an acute accent " ´ " to those vowels "e" and "o". If the word ends in "il", just add an "s" to the word because the "i" is already there.

- Canal (canal) = canais
- Azul (blue) = azuis
- Anel (ring) = anéis
- Lençol (sheet) = lençóis
- Canil (dog pound) = canis

➤ **Words ending in "em":**

With words that end in "em", you take off the "m" and add "ns". If a word has an acute accent on the "é", you carry the accent to the plural form. For instance:

- Garagem (garage) = garagens
- Refém (hostage) = reféns

➤ **Words ending in "r", "s" or "z":**

With words that end in either "r", "s", or "z", you just add an "es" to the end of the word. Like so:

- Motor (motor) = motores
- Luz (light) = luzes

- Português (portuguese) = portugueses[1]
- Mês (month) = meses
> **Words ending in "ão":**

With words that end in "ão", there can be three different possibilities to form the plural. These are the options: "ões", "ães", and "ãos". There is no rule that you can follow every time. What is more usual is the "ões", but the only way for you to know which one to use is to memorize them. Don't worry about that—you'll get there with practice. Here are some examples:

- Leão (lion) = leões
- Coração (heart) = corações
- Capitão (captain) = capitães
- Pão (bread) = pães
- Mão (hand) = mãos
- Orgão (organ) = orgãos

Once again, several rules can help when trying to turn a singular into a plural. However, and as you know by now, rules don't always apply. So you really need to watch out for some odd cases and try to memorize them. Below, you'll find a list of some exceptions to the rules previously mentioned, to which you can come back to whenever you need to make sure what is the correct way to write a word—either in its plural or singular form.

For instance, just like in English, some words are always used in the plural form (the article that precedes the noun is also in its plural form):

- Glasses – (os) Óculos
- Pants – (as) Calças
- Sneakers – (os) Ténis

---

[1] Tip: whenever you come across a word ending in "s", in which the letter immediately before the "s" has a diacritical mark, you just need to add the "es" and take out the diacritical mark to use it in its plural form, as shown in the examples above.

Then there are words in Portuguese that are only used in their plural form, but they don't correspond to their translation in English:

- (ir de) Férias – (going on) Vacation
- (as) Costas – Back (body part)

Some words that end in "s" don't have a plural form, so they don't change when you're referring to more than one of that. For instance:

- 1 lápis (1 pencil) = 2 lápis
- 1 vírus (1 virus) = 2 vírus
- 1 atlas (1 atlas) = 2 atlas

Exercise

1) **Let's test what you just learned. Write down the plural form of the following words:**

a) Sabor
b) Sabonete
c) Grão
d) Cão
e) Carrocel
f) Anzol
g) Sul
h) Paisagem
i) Limão
j) País
k) Armazém
l) Juvenil
m) Mãe
n) Pires
o) Céu
p) Sobral
q) Giz

Answers

1) Plural:

a) Sabores

b) Sabonetes

c) Grãos

d) Cães

e) Carrocéis

f) Anzóis

g) Suis

h) Paisagens

i) Limões

j) Países

k) Armazéns

l) Juvenis

m) Mães

n) Pires

o) Céus

p) Sobrais

q) Gizes

Gender in Portuguese

As we stated before, words in Portuguese have a gender. That applies to nouns, adjectives, and definite and indefinite articles. In this chapter, we will go more in depth about the nouns' genders. Below, in the Adjectives chapter, we will also see some examples of how gender affects them. For now, we will focus on nouns. Let's see what this is all about.

➤ Masculine and feminine nouns:

Nouns are words which are used to label objects, animals or people. In Portuguese, there is no neutral gender—a noun will always be either feminine or masculine. There is one general rule that will help you identify the gender of the word the great majority of the time. Masculine words tend to end with an "o", whereas feminine nouns tend to end in an "a". The article that precedes the noun will also be of great help since it follows this rule. For instance:

- A faca – the knife

- O saco – the bag

However, some nouns don't follow the rule. Some nouns end in an "a" but are masculine. For example:

- O chá – the tea
- O gorila – the gorilla

> **Nouns ending in an "e":**

Many nouns ending in an "e" are masculine in gender. Take a look at this example:

- O café – the coffee
- O telefone – the telephone

However, some of them may have a feminine correspondent. That happens when the noun refers to a person or an animal, which obviously can be either masculine or feminine. The gender of a noun can be easily modified by simply changing the definite article that precedes the noun. The word is actually spelled the same way for both genders, but the article before it determines if it's masculine or feminine.

- O estudante – the male student
- A estudante – the female student
- A (mulher) árabe – the female arabian
- O (homem) árabe – the male arabian

There are obviously some exceptions. There are words which end in "e" that are only feminine. Take a look at some of those:

- A estante – the bookcase
- A corrente – the current
- A lebre – the hare
- **Nouns ending in "ão":**

Most nouns ending in "ão" are masculine, but some feminine nouns end in "ão" as well:

- O ladrão – the thief
- O limão – the lemon

- O pão – the bread
- O coração – the heart
- A canção – the song
- A mão – the hand

Nouns ending in "em":

Nouns ending in "em" can be either masculine or feminine but tend to be more feminine. Don't forget that nouns that refer to people are spelled the same way for both genders, and it's the article that precedes it that will distinguish which gender they are:

- O jovem – the young man
- A jovem – the young woman
- O refém – the male hostage
- A refém – the female hostage
- A mensagem – the message
- A miragem – the mirage

Nouns ending in "or":

As for the nouns ending in "or", they can also be either masculine or feminine:

- O calor – the heat
- O cantor – the singer
- O louvor – the praise
- A flor – the flower
- A dor – the pain

Nouns ending in "iz"

Once again, nouns ending in "iz" can either be masculine or feminine:

- O nariz – the nose

- A raiz – the root
- O verniz (das unhas) – (nail) varnish
- A imperatriz – the empress

- **Nouns ending in "el" and "eu":**

In this situation, there are no doubts—every noun that ends in either "el" or "eu" is masculine. Take a look at a few examples:

- O anel – the ring
- O mel – the honey
- O papel – the paper
- O céu – the sky/heaven
- O chapéu – the hat
- O réu – the defendant
- O véu – the veil

Exercise

1) Write down the feminine of each noun:

a) Conde

b) Patrão

c) Herói

d) Ladrão

e) Ateu

f) Actor

2) Choose the option in which every noun is masculine:

a) Profeta, assombração, fantasma;

b) Profeta, telefonema, fantasma;

c) Eclipse, alface, champanhe;

d) Assombração, mascote, grama;

3) Write down which nouns are feminine and which ones are masculine:

a) Tigresa ( )

b) Marido ( )

c) Poeta ( )

d) Irmã ( )

e) Teia ( )

f) Ré ( )

4) Rewrite the sentence in the masculine form:

a) A minha afilhada foi testemunha de um caso.

b) A ré apresentou-se no tribunal.

c) A judia chegou cedo ao encontro.

d) A baronesa falou com a rainha.

Answers

1) a) condessa; b) patroa; c) heroína; d) ladra; e) ateia f) actriz.

2) The correct answer is b).

3) a) F; b) M; c) M; d) F; e) F; f) F

4) a) O meu afilhado foi testemunha de um caso.

b) O réu apresentou-se no tribunal.

c) O judeu chegou cedo ao encontro.

d) O barão falou com o rei.

Capitalization

There are some differences between the English and the Portuguese language when it comes to the capitalization, or not, of some words. To make it clearer for you, we are going to write down the most important situations in which lowercase should be used, and the most important situations in which uppercase is the rule.

You should use lowercase when referring to:

- Common use of everyday vocabulary;
- Days of the week, months, seasons[2];
- Cardinal points, but not when they are abbreviated[3];

You should use uppercase when referring to:

- People's names;
- Cities, Countries;
- First word of a sentence;
- In nouns that refer to institutes or associations;
- Holidays and festive activities;
- Book titles;
- Acronyms.

Exercise

1) Let's test what you just learned. Which of the following should start with a capital letter?

a) pedro

b) sul

c) sudoeste

d) verão

e) grã-bretanha

f) mesa

g) grão

h) itália

i) se (sudeste)

j) terça-feira

---

[2] This is the rule after the 1990 Orthographic Agreement. As stated before, we are following the rules prior to the Agreement (and as you'll see, whenever any of these words come up throughout the book, they will be written in uppercase), but we thought it was important to make you aware of this.

[3] The same as with the days of the week, months, and seasons—before the New Orthographic Agreement, these words were written in uppercase.

k) dezembro
l) lisboa
m) inverno
n) peta (the animals association)
o) domingo
p) natal

1) The correct answers are a); e); h); i); l); n); p).

Chapter 2 – The Fundamentals

Grammar rules

Word order

You may have noticed by now that the word order in the Portuguese language is different from the word order in English. And that's true in several situations. You may also have realized that whereas in English you say, "Maria has a beautiful car", a Portuguese native speaker would, literally translated, instead say that "Maria has a car beautiful". The good news is that generally speaking, the structure of a sentence in Portuguese is not much different from the one in English. You only have to pay attention to specific cases. The Portuguese word order is **Subject > Verb > Object.** Let's see how that works in different phrase formations.

➢ In a statement:

If your sentence is a statement, you are expressing a fact. Normally, you are talking about a specific event. Let's analyze the following sentences in pairs—first the Portuguese and then the English ones, sentence by sentence. Please compare and contrast the Portuguese word order and the English one carefully.

Subject (s) > Verb (v) > Object (o) > Phrase Complement (pc)

- He has a house in Rio de Janeiro. – Ele (s) tem (v) uma casa (o) no Rio de Janeiro (pc).
- She washed her clothes in the washing machine. – Ela (s) lavou (v) a roupa (o) na máquina de lavar (pc).
- We read a book at the beach. – Nós (s) lemos (v) um livro (o) na praia (pc).
- They have salmon for lunch. – Eles (s) comem (v) salmão (o) ao almoço (pc).
- You sirs are going to schedule the meeting for tomorrow. – Os senhores (s) vão marcar (v) a reunião (o) para amanhã (pc).

Please be aware that when speaking in Portuguese, the subject is often hidden. This is something that was talked about in the "A Few Tips about Portuguese" chapter. What this means is that the verb itself indicates the subject of that sentence. For instance, instead of "Nós vamos à escola amanhã" (We are going to school tomorrow), it can simply be "*Vamos* à escola amanhã."

➢ In a description:

The descriptive word, or in other words, the adjective, usually needs to be placed after the noun. Let's see what this is all about with some examples:

Subject > Adjective 1 > Verb > Adjective 2

- The big house is beautiful. – A casa (s) grande (a1) é (v) bonita (a2).
- The ripe bananas are cheaper. – As bananas (s) maduras (a1) são (v) mais baratas (a2).
- An old car isn't expensive. – Um carro (s) velho (a1) não é (v) caro (a2).
- Wide streets are less dangerous. – Ruas (s) largas (a1) são (v) menos perigosas (a2).
- The new computer ended up more expensive. – O computador (s) novo (a1) ficou (v) mais caro (a2).

➤ In a statement-question:

If you want to ask a question in Portuguese, the Portuguese word order is the same as when you make a statement. All you have to do is to raise the intonation at the end to make it sound like a question. However, pay attention to the fact that whereas in English you need to use a verb at the beginning when you ask a question, in Portuguese you don't need to. So, if it helps, when you are transferring your thoughts from English into Portuguese, try to imagine that you could ask questions in English without the words "do", "are" or "will", etc., at the beginning of a question. For instance, in English, you would say "Are you gentlemen going to schedule a meeting for tomorrow?" whereas in Portuguese you would say "Os senhores vão marcar a reunião para amanhã?". For you to understand the correct Portuguese word order, let's observe the same phrases used above as examples, now turned into questions.

Subject > Verb > Object > Phrase Complement

- Does he have a house in Rio de Janeiro? – Ele (s) tem (v) uma casa (o) no Rio de Janeiro (pc)?
- Did she wash her clothes in the washing machine? – Ela (s) lavou (v) a roupa (o) na máquina de lavar (pc)?
- Did we read a book at the beach? – Nós (s) lemos (v) um livro (o) na praia (pc)?
- Are they having salmon for lunch? – Eles (s) comem (v) salmão (o) ao almoço (pc)?

➤ In a direct question:

You basically keep the normal structure of a statement, then adding a question word at the beginning, and obviously raising the intonation at the end. Let's, once again, look at some examples.

Subject > Verb > Object

- What does he do in Rio de Janeiro? – O que (é que) ele (s) faz (v) no Rio de Janeiro (o)?

- Where did she wash her clothes? – Onde (é que) ela (s) lavou (v) a roupa (o)?
- Where do we read the book? – Onde (é que) nós (s) lemos (v) o livro (o)?
- What do they have for lunch? – O que (é que) eles (s) comem (v) ao almoço (o)?

➢ In negative form:

What you need to do to form a negative sentence is to place the negative word before the verb to get a correct Portuguese word order. Negative words are often "não" (no, don't), "nunca" (never), or "nem" (nor). Nevertheless, remember: the word order in Portuguese is still the same.

Subject > Negative locution > Verb > Object

- I don't want soup. – Eu (s) não (nl) quero (v) sopa (o).
- He never studied the word order. – Ele (s) nunca (nl) estudou (v) a ordem das palavras (o).
- We aren't going to the beach. – Nós (s) não (nl) vamos (v) à praia (o).
- They are not even going to have lunch at home. – Eles (s) nem (nl) vão (v) almoçar em casa (o).
- The milk is never fresh. – O leite (s) nunca (nl) é fresco (o).

Exercise

1) Translate these sentences to Portuguese:

a) What is your dog's name?

b) My dad has a green shirt.

c) I don't have a good laptop for gaming.

d) I want the vegetable soup.

2) Ask the direct questions that originated these sentences
(E.g.: I prefer the strawberry ice cream. Which ice cream do you

prefer? = Eu prefiro o gelado de morango. – Qual é o gelado que preferes?):

a) Eu vou à escola amanhã.

b) É o meu pai que te vai buscar ao cinema.

c) Eu sei isso porque estudei.

d) A minha cor favorita é azul.

3) Write these sentences in the negative form:

a) Eu quero ir correr!

b) Tu gostas de camarão?

c) Eles vêm connosco à praia.

d) Vocês fazem sempre o que vos peço.

e) Eu até sei muito sobre esse assunto.

Answers

2) Translations:

a) Qual é o nome do teu cão?

b) O meu pai tem uma camisa verde.

c) Eu não tenho um computador bom para jogos.

d) Eu quero a sopa de vegetais.

3) Questions4:

e) Quando vais à escola?

f) Quem me vai buscar ao cinema?

g) Como sabes isso?

h) Qual é a tua cor favorita?

4) Negative:

i) Eu não quero ir correr.

j) Tu não gostas de camarão?

---

[4] The solution to this exercise presents some examples that are accepted; there are, however, many other possible answers.

k) Eles não vêm connosco à praia.

l) Vocês nunca fazem o que vos peço. / Vocês fazem sempre o que não vos peço.

m) Eu até nem sei muito sobre esse assunto.

Determiners

The determiners are elements of the language which are placed before the noun and that identify or determine what the noun refers to. They differ from the pronouns in the sense that pronouns substitute nouns, whereas determiners, as said previously, precede them. Check out this example, so it becomes clearer:

- A *minha* mãe é alta! – My mom is tall!
- A *minha* também é! – Mine is as well!

In the first sentence, the word "minha" precede the noun "mãe"; therefore it is a determiner. In the second sentence, the word "minha" works as a substitute for "mãe"; hence it is a pronoun.

There are six different types of determiners, and we are going to study them all. Bear in mind that in Portuguese, the determiners must agree in gender and number with the noun. Later on, we will also approach the pronouns to see how to use and identify them. Be aware that many words are used both as determiners and pronouns, depending on the context. So, whenever you're doing some reading, try to identify the noun in the sentence, so you can more accurately determine what the word is referring to.

➢ **Possessive determiners:**
- Meu / minha (my); meus / minhas;
- Teu / tua (your); teus /tuas;
- Seu / sua (her/his); seus / suas;
- Nosso; nossa (our) / nossos; nossas;
- Vosso / vossa (your); vossos; vossas;
- Seu / sua (their); seus /suas.

These exist to indicate possession regarding someone or something. For instance:

- My shirt is blue. – A *minha* camisa é azul.

➢ Demonstrative determiners:

- Este / esta (this); estes / estas (these);
- Esse / essa (that); esses / essas (those);
- Aquele / aquela (that); aqueles /aquelas (those);
- Isto (this, or this thing right here);
- Isso (that, or that thing – further away than "this", but closer than "aquilo");
- Aquilo (that thing over there).

These exist to identify and indicate the position, whether in time or space, of someone or something. For instance:

- This is my house. – Esta é a minha casa.

➢ Indefinite determiners[5]:

- Todo / toda (all); todos / todas;
- Algum / alguma (any, something); alguns / algumas (some);
- Nenhum/ nenhuma (none); nenhuns / nenhumas;
- Outro / outra (other); outros / outras (others);
- Muito / muita (a lot, many, quite); muitos / muitas (many);
- Pouco / pouca (little, not much); poucos / poucas (few);
- Tanto / tanta (much/such); tantos / tantas (many);
- Qualquer (any); quaisquer;
- Tudo (everything);
- Nada (nothing);
- Cada (each);
- Ninguém (no one/nobody);
- Alguém (someone/somebody).

---

[5] The English translations to the indefinite determiners are not totally accurate, at least not for every situation—since the English word might change depending on what is being said, even if the Portuguese term is the same in those different sentences.

These exist to refer to being or things in an imprecise way. For instance:

- I'm going to call somebody to come here. – Vou chamar alguém para vir cá.

➤ Quantifiers and interrogative determiners:

- Qual (which one); quais (which ones);
- Quanto / quanta (how much); quantos / quantas (how many);
- Que (what);
- Quem (who, whom).

These exist to introduce interrogations, or when we're in need of giving someone information about the number or amount of something. For instance:

- What is the price? – Qual é o preço?
- How many flowers are in the jar? – Quantas flores estão no jarro?

➤ Pre-determiners:

- Cujo / cuja (which); cujos/ cujas (whose);
- Quanto / quanta (how much); quantos/ quantas (how many);
- Qual (which); quais (which ones);
- Que (what);
- Quem (who, whom).

These are used to express the opinion about the noun they modify. For instance:

- What a sunny day! – *Que* dia tão solarengo!

Articles

The determiners "the", and "a" or "an" are translated to Portuguese as "o", "a", "os", "as" and "um", "uma", "uns", "umas". Language experts call these words "articles", which are words that come before nouns and are used to define their gender. In

Portuguese, just like in the English language, there are two types of articles: the definite articles—"o", "a", "os", "as"—and the indefinite articles—"um", "uma", "uns", and "umas". The reason that there are four representations of both types of articles in Portuguese is because there is a distinction between the masculine and feminine words, and between the singular and plural. Let's see how they are used in some sentences.

➤ The definite article:

The definite article implies that something is one thing, or a specific thing, or several specific things. It is, as the name implies, something that is defined or determined already. In Portuguese, the word "o" corresponds to a masculine singular noun, and the word "os" corresponds to a masculine, plural noun, where the word "a" corresponds to a feminine singular noun, and the word "as" corresponds to a feminine plural noun:

- O bolo de aniversário – The birthday cake.
- Os bolos de aniversário – The birthday cakes
- A bola de futebol – The soccer ball
- As bolas de futebol – The soccer balls

➤ The indefinite article:

The indefinite article implies that something is one undetermined or unspecified thing, among others of the same kind. The word "um" corresponds to a masculine, singular noun, and the word "uns" corresponds to a masculine, plural noun, whereas the word "uma" corresponds to a feminine, singular noun, and the word "umas" corresponds to a feminine, plural noun.

- Um bolo de aniversário – A birthday cake
- Uns bolos de aniversário – Some birthday cakes
- Uma bola de futebol – A soccer ball
- Umas bolas de futebol – Some soccer balls

Exercise

1) Identify the determiners in the following sentences:

a) O jardineiro tratou do meu jardim.

b) Estas flores exigem cuidados.

c) Aquela fila do teatro está reservada para a nossa equipa.

d) Que trabalho vais fazer?

2) Fill in the blanks with either definite or indefinite articles:

a) Fui ao cinema e vi _____ bom filme. Estava lá _____ meu amigo João, que me convidou para ir ver _____ filme, que era _____ filme preferido dele. _____ meus amigos da escola queriam ver outra coisa, então foram para _____ casa da Maria. Ela preparou _____ tostas com queijo.

3) Which sentences have a determiner on it? Write down the determiner:

a) Eu gosto muito dele.

b) Aquela casa é a minha.

c) Este é o meu irmão.

d) O jardineiro tratou-me disso.

Answers

1) a) meu; b) estas; c) aquela, nossa; d) que

2) a) Fui ao cinema e vi *um* bom filme. Estava lá *o* meu amigo João, que me convidou para ir ver *um* filme, que era *o* filme preferido dele. *Os* meus amigos da escola queriam ver outra coisa, então foram para *a* casa da Maria. Ela preparou *umas* tostas com queijo.

3) b) aquela; c) meu

Verbs and Tenses

In Portuguese, verbs are conjugated according to their endings. There are three different ways of conjugating them:

- The first form or conjugation includes all regular verbs ending in "ar";
- The second conjugation includes all regular verbs ending in "er";
- And the third conjugation includes all regular verbs ending in "ir".

As in any other language, there are also irregular verbs in Portuguese, which are not included in those three ways of conjugating verbs. To conjugate a verb in the present tense you take the verb, separate the stem (take out its ending—"ar", "er", or "ir"), and then you add the endings which are specific for this tense.

A quick, and *extremely important*, note before we start: the two verbs "**ser**" and "**estar**" are both a translation of to the verb "to be" in English, but each verb is used in different situations. The difference lies in the fact that "**ser**" is used, generally, when we are referring to more permanent states. For example, to talk about height, type of body, nationality, and things of this nature, i.e., things that are unlikely[6] to change in our lives, the verb "**ser**" is used. On the other hand, if you are talking about states that are likely to suffer changes, the verb "**estar**" is used. If you want to say something about the way you feel at a certain moment, how the weather is on a specific day, or other things that will probably change in no time, you'll use this form of the verb "to be". Let's take a look at a few examples:

- Eu sou alta. – I am tall.
- Eu estou contente. – I am happy.

---

[6] Just a fun fact – if you want to say "I'm married" in Portuguese, you would have to use the verb "ser" – "Eu *sou* casado/a". And that is because even though it is not a permanent state, historically, once you got married, that likely wouldn't ever change.

- Eu sou loira. – I am blonde.
- Eu tenho 20 anos. – I am 20 years old.

Present Tense

➢ Verbs ending in "ar":

For the verbs ending in "ar", you add the following endings to their stem—"o", "as", "a", "amos", "ais", and "am". For instance:

- Verb "to love" – amar, stem – am;
  - o Present of amar: Eu amo, Tu amas, Ele/ela ama, Nós amamos, Vós[7] amais, Eles amam;
- Verb "to sing" – cantar, stem – cant;
  - o Present of cantar: Eu canto, Tu cantas, Ele/ela canta, Nós cantamos, Vós cantais, cantam;
- Verb "to speak" – falar, stem – fal;
  - o Present of falar: Eu falo, Tu falas, Ele/ela fala, Nós falamos, Vós falais, Eles falam.

➢ Verbs ending in "er":

For the verbs that end in "er" in the present tense, you add the following endings to their stem—"o", "es", "e", "emos", "eis", and "em". For instance:

- Verb "to eat" – comer, stem – com;
- Present of comer: Eu como, Tu comes, Ele/ela come, Nós comemos, Vós comeis, Eles comem;
- Verb "to live" – viver, stem – viv;
- Present of viver: Eu vivo, Tu vives, Ele/ela vive, Nós vivemos, Vós viveis, Eles vivem;
- Verb "to fear" – temer, stem – tem;
- Present of temer: Eu temo, Tu temes, Ele/ela teme, Nós tememos, Vós temeis, Eles temem.

---

[7] "Vós", which corresponds to the second person plural, is rarely used nowadays. What you will hear 99% of the times in written and/or spoken form is the word "vocês", which means the same thing. However, there's a catch—if you use "vocês", you have to conjugate the verb as if it were in the third person plural.

> ## Verbs ending in "ir":

To conjugate the verbs that end in "ir" in the present tense, you add the following endings to their stem—"o", "es", "e", "imos", "is", and "em". For instance:

- Verb "to leave" – partir, stem – part;
- Present of partir: Eu parto, Tu partes, Ele/ela parte, Nós partimos, Vós partis, Eles partem;
- Verb "to insist" – insistir, stem – insist;
- Present of insistir: Eu insisto, Tu insistes, Ele/ela insiste, Nós insistimos, Vós insistis, Eles insistem;
- Verb "to fullfil" – cumprir, stem –cumpr;
- Present of cumprir: Eu cumpro, Tu cumpres, Ele/ela cumpre, Nós cumprimos, Vós cumpris, Eles cumprem.

Past Tense

Now, we are going to focus on the Past Simple tense, referred to in Portuguese as "passado perfeito", which is used to refer to actions that happened or were completed in the recent past. The Past Simple refers to completed actions that had a definite beginning and a definite end. As you know by now, in Portuguese there are three different classes of verbs: the verbs ending in "ar", the verbs ending in "er", and the verbs ending in "ir". Each class of regular verbs has its own pattern of termination when conjugated in the past. When conjugating regular verbs in the simple past form, you just have to preserve the root of the verb and substitute "ar", "er" or "ir" for the following terminations:

- Verb "to love" – amar, stem – am
  - o Past simple of amar: Eu amei, Tu amaste, Ele/ela amou, Nós amámos, Vós amastes, Eles amaram;
- Verb "to run" – correr, stem – corr;
  - o Past simple of correr: Eu corri, Tu correste, Ele/ela correu, Nós corremos, Vós correstes, Eles correram;
- Verb "to feel" – sentir, stem – sent;

o Past simple of sentir: Eu senti, Tu sentiste, Ele/ela sentiu, Nós sentimos, Vós sentistes, Eles sentiram;

For verbs ending in "gar" and "car", the first person—"eu"—is conjugated using the termination "guei" and"quei", as you can see in the following examples:

- Verb "to arrive" – chegar, stem – cheg;
  o Past simple of chegar: Eu cheguei, Tu chegaste, Ele/ela chegou, Nós chegámos, Vós chegastes, Eles chegaram;
- Verb "to stay" – ficar, stem – fic;
  o Past simple of ficar: Eu fiquei, Tu ficaste, Ele/ela ficou, Nós ficámos, Vós ficastes, Eles ficaram;

Future Tense

Let's switch to the future now. The simplest of all of the future tenses is simply known as 'future' or 'future of the indicative', which is the one we are going to study for now. In English, this tense is achieved by using the auxiliary verb "will", or sometimes "shall". In Portuguese, however, the future tense is not used very often in oral communication, especially if it is informal. You are more likely to come across the future indicative in writing than in speech. The true future indicative is a simple form, and is conjugated as follows:

- Verb "to work" – trabalhar, stem – trabalh
  o Future indicative of trabalhar: Eu trabalharei, Tu trabalharás, Ele/ela trabalhará, Nós trabalharemos, Vós trabalhareis, Eles trabalharão;
- Verb "to think" – pensar, stem – pens;
  o Future indicative of pensar: Eu pensarei, Tu pensarás, Ele/ela pensará, Nós pensaremos, Vós pensareis, Eles pensarão;
- Verb "to eat" – comer, stem – com;
  o Future indicative of comer: Eu comerei, Tu comerás, Ele/ela comerá, Nós comeremos, Vós comereis, Eles comerão;

- Verb "to write" – escrever, stem – escrev
  - Future indicative of escrever: Eu escreverei, Tu escreverás, Ele/ela escreverá, Nós escreveremos, Vós escrevereis, Eles escreverão;
- Verb "to guarantee" – garantir, stem – garant;
  - Future indicative of garantir: Eu garantirei, Tu garantirás, Ele/ela garantirá, Nós garantiremos, Vós garantireis, Eles garantirão;
- Verb "to attend" – assistir, stem – assist;
  - Future indicative of assistir: Eu assistirei, Tu assistirás, Ele/ela assistirá, Nós assistiremos, Vós assistireis, Eles assistirão;

However, not all verbs follow these rules. Here are a few examples of the conjugation of irregular verbs:

- Verb "to be" – estar, stem – est
  - Future indicative of estar: Eu estarei, Tu estarás, Ele/ela estará, Nós estaremos, Vós estareis, Eles estarão;
- Verb "to be" – ser, stem – ser;
  - Future indicative of ser: Eu serei, Tu serás, Ele/ela será, Nós seremos, Vós sereis, Eles serão;
- Verb "to go" – ir, stem – ir;
  - Future indicative of ir: Eu irei, Tu irás, Ele/ela irá, Nós iremos, Vós ireis, Eles irão;

A helpful hint for remembering the future indicative forms is that they all start with the full infinitive—not just the stem of it (although not all irregular verbs do so). Be careful, though, not to confuse the third person plural form of the future indicative with the past third person plural, as they both start with the full infinitive.

Exercise

1) **Conjugate the verb "lançar" in the present tense.**

2) **Conjugate the verb "beber" in the future tense.**

3) Conjugate the verb "sorrir" in the simple past tense.

4) Rewrite these sentences in the simple past tense:

a) Eu como um gelado.

b) Eu gosto muito deste filme.

c) Ele não morre tão facilmente.

5) Rewrite these sentences in the future tense:

a) Eu vou à praia amanhã.

b) Ele está preparado par ao teste.

c) Nós fazemos isto.

Answers

1) Eu lanço, tu lanças, ele/ela lança, nós lançamos, vós lançais, eles lançam.

2) Eu beberei, tu beberás, ele/ela beberá, nós beberemos, vós bebereis, eles beberão.

3) Eu sorri, tu sorriste, ele/ela sorriu, nós sorrimos, vós sorristes, eles sorriram.

4) a) Eu comi um gelado. b) Eu gostei muito deste filme. c) Ele não morreu tão facilmente.

5) a) Eu irei à praia amanhã. b) Ele estará preparado para o teste. c) Nós faremos isto.

Adjectives

In Portuguese, an adjective must agree in gender and number with the word it is describing. Most of the time it is accompanied by a form of the verb "to be": either "ser" or "estar". Therefore, when you want to use an adjective to describe a word in Portuguese, you need to take into consideration whether it's in the masculine or feminine form and whether it's in the plural or singular, to then make the necessary adjustment—if any is needed. Another thing to consider is the form of the verb you're going to use. If you're describing an intrinsic quality or characteristic—which is something that is part of the noun you're talking about—you need to use the verb "ser". If you're describing a temporary condition or state of the noun you're talking about, you need to use the verb "estar".

> Here are some examples of an intrinsic quality:
>   - The blanket is green. – A manta *é* verde.
>   - João is stubborn. – O João *é* teimoso.
>   - Carla is stubborn. – A Carla é teimosa.
>   - Marina's eyes are blue. – Os olhos da Marina são azuis.
> Here are some examples of a temporary condition or state:
>   - The children are sick. – As crianças estão doentes.
>   - The dog is happy. – O cão está alegre.
>   - I am not okay. – Eu não estou bem.

Adverbs

An adverb is a word that can modify or characterize an action. In Portuguese, adverbs are varied in their forms and context to express time, place, mode, quantity, intensity, affirmation, denial, doubt and exclusivity. They can modify and adapt to:

  - A verb;
  - An adjective;
  - Another adverb.

Now we will give you a small list of several adverbs from the different types mentioned above. It would obviously be impossible to name them all, especially with Portuguese being such a rich language, but adverbs are very important since they help you express yourself and get your message across in a much more effective way. Reading will definitely help you master these.

> **Adverbs that indicate time**:
>   - Immediately – Imediatemente
>   - Constantly – Constantemente
> **Adverbs that indicate place:**

- Here – Aqui
- Above – Acima
> **Adverbs that indicate mode or manner:**
  - Quickly – Depressa/Rapidamente
  - Easily – Facilmente
> **Adverbs that indicate quantity or intensity:**
  - Very– Muito
  - Little – Pouco
  - More – Mais
  - Less – Menos
> **Adverbs that indicate affirmation:**
  - Certainly – Certamente
  - Surely – Decerto
> **Adverbs that indicate denial:**
  - Never – Nunca
  - Neither – Nem
  - Never ever – Jamais
> **Adverbs that indicate doubt:**
  - Maybe – Talvez
  - Probably – Provavelmente
> **Adverbs that indicate exclusivity:**
Only – Somente
  - Otherwise – SenãoPronouns

Pronouns exist to replace other words, either names or nouns. A pronoun, when used, makes your speech and conversation sound more natural and fluent, and at the same time, it breaks the boredom of repetition and redundancy. For instance, when you are introduced to somebody by a friend, you may have learned that you must say "Prazer em conhecê-lo/a", which means "Nice to meet you". In this case, the letters "lo/la" substitute the name of the person that you are referring to—so that is one example of a personal pronoun.

There are many different types of pronouns—the same types that there are in the determiners' category. We are going to, however, focus on the personal pronouns, more specifically in the direct object pronouns, and the indirect object pronouns, for now, to know how to use those and identify them in sentences.

➢ Personal pronouns:
o Direct object pronouns:

These are the pronouns that will lead you to the questions: "what" – "o quê" –, and "who" – "quem". For instance, take a look at this sentence:

- I'm dating Pedro. – Eu estou a namorar com o Pedro.

In this situation, you would ask "who are you dating?" The answer would be "Pedro." So that's the noun you are going to substitute for the pronoun. It would look like this:

- I'm dating him. – Eu estou a namorar com ele.

There are only eight pronouns under the direct object pronouns category:

- "Me" = which corresponds to the word "me" in English;
- "Te" = which corresponds to the word "you" in English;
- "O" = which corresponds to the word "him" or "it" when the object is masculine;
- "A" = which corresponds to the word "her" or "it" when the object is feminine;
- "Nos" = which corresponds to the word "us";
- "Vos", or "Vocês" = which corresponds to the plural of "you", just like the expression "you guys";
- "Os" = which corresponds to a masculine "them", be it people or objects;
- "As" = which also corresponds to a feminine "them" in English, be it people or objects.

Here are some rules to follow almost all of the time:

1) The pronoun comes after the verb, separated by a hyphen. For instance:

- I ate all of the ice cream. – Eu comi o gelado todo. = Eu comi-o todo.

2) The pronoun needs to be placed before the verb when the verb comes after, in five different situations:

- o **Adverbs** – I also ate the ice cream. – Eu **também** comi o gelado = Eu também *o* comi.

- o **Negatives** – I didn't eat the ice cream. – Eu **não** comi o gelado. = Eu não *o* comi.

- o **Interrogations** – Who ate the ice cream? – **Quem** comeu o gelado? = Quem *o* comeu?

- o **Relative pronouns** – He said he ate all of the ice cream. – Ele disse **que** comeu o gelado todo. = Ele disse que *o* comeu todo.

- o **Prepositions** – She likes eating the ice cream with a spoon. – Ela gosta **de** comer o gelado com uma colher. = Ela gosta de *o* comer com uma colher.

3) If the verb ends with the letters "s", "z", or "r", the last letters of the verb fall and you add an "l" to the beginning of the pronouns "o" "a", "os" or "as". For instance:

- I'm going to do the portrait. – Eu vou fazer o retrato. = Eu vou fazê-*lo*.

4) When the verb ends with a nasal sound, keep the verb as it is and add "n" to the pronoun. For instance:

- They drink all of the wine. – Eles bebem o vinho todo = Eles bebem-*no* todo"

o **Indirect object pronouns:**

These are the pronouns that will lead you to the question "to whom", which in Portuguese has two forms – "A quem" and "Para quem". Bear in mind that if you're not able to ask "a quem" or "para quem", (to whom), and instead, the pronoun leads you to the question "quem" (who), you're not dealing with an indirect object, but instead with a direct object.

Again, we only have eight indirect object pronouns. Here they are:

- "Me"= which corresponds to the words "to me" in English;

- "Te"= which corresponds to the words "to you" in English;
- "Lhe"= which corresponds to the words "to him" or "to it" when the object is masculine;
- "Lhe"= which corresponds to the words "to her" or "to it" when the object is feminine;
- "Nos"= which corresponds to the words "to us";
- "Vos", or "para vocês" = which corresponds to the plural "to you", just like the expression "to you guys";
- "Lhes"= which corresponds to a masculine "to them", whether it is referring to people or objects;
- "Lhes" = which corresponds to a feminine "to them", whether it is referring to people or objects.

These obey the same rules the direct object pronouns do in terms of where they are placed in a sentence—whether it is before or after the verb. In other words, they normally come after the verb separated by a hyphen. For instance:

- I'm going to give Mário the book. – Eu vou dar o livro ao Mário. = Eu vou-lhe dar o livro.

The exceptions—when pronouns come before the verb—are also the same as before, and that happens when we have:

1) Adverbs:
   a) I also called Paulo. – Eu **também** telefonei para o Paulo. = Eu também *lhe* telefonei.

2) Negative statements:
   a) He doesn't call Paulo. – Ele **não** telefona para o Paulo. = Ele não *lhe* telefona.

3) Interrogations:
   a) Who called Paulo today? – **Quem** telefonou para o Paulo hoje? = Quem *lhe* telefonou hoje?

4) Relative pronouns:
   a) He said he hit Pedro. – Ele disse **que** bateu no Pedro. = Ele disse que *lhe* bateu.

5) Prepositions:

a) She asked them to bring a coffee to him. – Ela disse **para** eles trazerem um café **para** ele. = Ela disse-*lhes* para *lhe* trazerem um café.

   o **Direct and indirect object pronouns:**

When we have both direct and indirect object pronouns together in a sentence, this is what you should do:

- He gave it to me. – Ele deu-me o livro. = Ele deu-mo.
- He gave it to you. – Ele deu-te o livro. = Ele deu-to.
- He gave it to him. – Ele deu-lhe o livro. = Ele deu-lho.

Exercise

1) **Complete the blank spaces with the definite object:**

   a) Eu vou preparar o jantar às sete da noite. – Eu vou … às sete da noite.

   b) Não vi os seus óculos. – Não … vi.

   c) Eles compraram os bilhetes hoje. – Eles … hoje.

   d) Vocês convidaram a Maria e o Carlos? – Vocês …?

   e) Eu fechei as janelas todas. – Eu … todas.

   f) Ele põe os pratos na mesa. – Ele … na mesa.

   g) Ela já leu o jornal? – Ela já …?

   h) Você quer fazer o exercício? – Você …?

   i) José comprou um presente ontem. – O José … ontem.

   j) Nós vimos as meninas na festa. – Nós … na festa.

2) **Complete the blank spaces with the indefinite object:**

   a) Quem disse isso ao Manuel e à Sofia? – Quem … isso?

   b) Ela trouxe esse livro para nós. – Ela … esse livro.

   c) Eles já entregaram a carta para a Maria? – Eles já … a carta?

   d) Nós demos um bonito presente de Natal ao José. – Nós … um bonito presente de Natal.

   e) A Maria ligou para você hoje às 3 horas. – A Maria … hoje às 3 horas.

3) Rewrite the whole sentences using the pronouns you know:

      a) O João trouxe-me o caderno hoje.

      b) A Catarina não vem fazer o bolo.

      c) Eu dei ao Carlos o presente anteontem.

      d) Os pintores pintaram a casa ontem.

6) Identify the pronouns and determiners in the following sentence:

      Esta casa é a minha casa. Aquela é a tua.

Answers

1) Definite object:

      a) Eu vou prepará-lo às sete da noite.

      b) Não os vi.

      c) Eles compraram-nos hoje.

      d) Vocês convidaram-nos?

      e) Eu fechei-as todas.

      f) Ele põe-nos na mesa.

      g) Ela já o leu?

      h) Você quer fazê-lo?

      i) O José comprou-o ontem.

      j) Nós vimo-las na festa.

2) Indefinite object:

      a) Quem lhes disse isso?

      b) Ela trouxe-nos esse livro.

      c) Eles já lhe entregaram a carta?

      d) Nós demos-lhe um bonito presente de Natal.

      e) A Maria ligou-lhe hoje às 3 horas.

3) Definite and indefinite object:

      a) Ele trouxe-mo hoje.

      b) Ela não o vem fazer.

      c) Eu dei-lho anteontem.

      d) Eles pintaram-na ontem.

4) Pronouns and determiners:

Esta – demonstrative determiner; Minha – possessive determiner;
Aquela – demonstrative pronoun; Tua – possessive pronoun

Chapter 3 – Short Stories
#1 – The Beginning

Foi num solarengo dia de verão que os irmãos, Ana e Francisco, entraram num táxi rumo à estação de comboios da Gare do Oriente. Era lá que se tinham combinado encontrar com o seu grupo de amigos para apanhar o comboio que os iria levar até às suas tão desejadas férias no Algarve. Chegaram finalmente à linha de onde o comboio iria partir, e o resto do grupo já estava todo à sua espera.

It was on a sunny summer day that the siblings, Ana and Francisco, got into a taxi headed to the train station Gare do Oriente. It was there that they were going to meet with their group of friends to catch the train that would take them to their desired holiday in the Algarve. They finally arrived at the line from which the train would leave, and the rest of the group was already waiting.

- Finalmente! Estava a ver que não chegavam a tempo – disse Mário, o namorado de Ana.
- Olá para ti também! – respondeu Ana com um sorriso, ao mesmo tempo que dava a Mário um abraço.
- Bom dia! Todos tranquilos que há muito tempo ainda! – atirou Francisco, sempre sem pressas.

- Bom dia não, é mais boa tarde! Têm sorte que o comboio também está atrasado e ainda não chegou. Devia estar aqui às 9h28, e já são 9h31. Costuma ser pontual, ao contrário de vocês. Mas desta vez a sorte esteve do vosso lado! É que se o perdessem, não tinham outra opção senão ir de autocarro. É que com a quantidade de gente que está aqui para ir para o Algarve hoje, não conseguiam bilhete de certeza! – exclamou Teresa.

- É verdade. O meu primo também vai ao festival e quis comprar bilhete para hoje à noite e já não havia nada. Só conseguiu para amanhã de manhã. – acrescentou Rui.

- Finally! I thought you'd not make it in time. – said Mário, Ana's boyfriend.

- Hello to you too! – Ana replied with a smile, at the same time giving Mário a hug.

- Good morning! Relax, there's still a lot of time! – said Francisco, always calm.

- Not good morning, it's almost good afternoon! You're lucky that the train is also late and has not yet arrived. It should have been here at 9:28 am, and it's now 9:31 am. It's usually on time, unlike you. But this time, luck was on your side! Because, if you had missed it, you would have no choice but to take the bus. And with the amount of people that are here to go to the Algarve today, you couldn't get a ticket! – said Teresa.

- That's true. My cousin is also going to the festival and wanted to buy a ticket for tonight, and there was nothing. He only managed to get one for tomorrow morning. – added Rui.

Este era um grupo de amigos que se conhecia de já há muito muito tempo. Os seus feitios, pese embora bastante diferentes, conjugavam muito bem entre si, o que fazia com que a sua amizade fosse verdadeira e muito pacífica, pelo menos a grande maioria das vezes. Tinham andados todos juntos na escola desde o ensino primário. Desde então nunca mais se quiseram separar. Depois de acabarem o

4°ano continuaram juntos, sempre na mesma escola e na mesma turma, pelo ensino secundário, e partilhando de interesses semelhantes, além de não suportarem a ideia de se separar, decidiram ir todos para a mesma licenciatura – a de Literatura Clássica – candidatando-se, naturalmente, para a mesma faculdade – a Faculdade de Letras da Universidade de Lisboa.

This was a group of friends who knew each other for a long time. Their personalities, although quite different, conjugated together very well among themselves, what caused their friendship to be genuine and very peaceful, at least the vast majority of the time. They all been in school together since first grade. Since then, they never wanted to go separate ways. After finishing the fourth grade, they continued together, always in the same school and in the same class in high school, and, due to sharing similar interests, and also because they couldn't stand the idea of separating, they then decided to take the same degree – Classic Literature – applying for, of course, the same college – the Faculty of Letters of the University of Lisbon.

A Ana e o Francisco eram irmãos gémeos. Surpreendentemente, sempre foram muito apegados um ao outro, e nunca tiveram a necessidade de se afastar. A sua relação era boa, com pequenas chatices e brigas, como é normal entre todos os irmãos, e eram muito cúmplices. No entanto, e apesar de serem gémeos, fisicamente não eram nada parecidos um ao outro. Ambos eram morenos, mas as suas semelhanças ficavam-se por aí. Ana tinha os olhos castanhos; Francisco tinha os olhos verdes claros. Francisco era alto e atlético; Ana baixa, e magra. Francisco tinha o nariz achatado, olhos em bico, e os lábios grossos e carnudos. Ana tinha os olhos grandes e redondos, o nariz pontiagudo, e a boca e lábios bem desenhados, mas finos. Quem os visse não adivinharia nunca que eram irmãos, quanto mais gémeos! Curioso era o facto de a Ana se parecer muito mais com a Teresa do que ao seu próprio irmão. Teresa tinha, tal como Ana, os olhos castanhos, mas ainda mais escuros. A Teresa também era baixa e magra, apesar de ser ligeiramente curvilínea. Também os seus narizes se assemelhavam bastante. Tinham as duas um nariz muito pontiagudo, embora não fosse comprido. O que definitivamente as distinguia era os seus cabelos: A Ana era morena, e tinha o cabelo liso e comprido. Teresa tinha uma farta, volumosa cabeleira loira, aos caracóis, que não passava do ombro. O Mário, o namorado de Ana, era o mais alto de todos do grupo. Ele não era gordo, mas tinha peso a mais. Os seus braços e pernas, tal como as suas mãos, eram longos. Usava óculos com uma lente tão grossa que os seus olhos aumentavam por detrás das lentes. O seu cabelo era preto, e parecia estar, impreterivelmente, sempre despenteado. O Rui, por outro lado, tinha um sedoso cabelo de cor castanha. O Rui era algo vaidoso, preocupava-se sempre em vestir-se bem, e estar bem arranjado. Era muito moreno, e os seus olhos eram pretos, de cor de azeitona.

Ana and Francisco were twins. Amazingly, they had always been very attached to each other, and never had the need to get away. Their relationship was good, with small troubles and fights, as it is normal between all brothers and sisters, and their chemistry was very good. However, and although they were twins, physically they weren't anything alike. Both were brunettes, but the similarities ended there. Ana had brown eyes; Francisco had light green eyes. Francisco was tall and athletic; Ana short and thin. Francisco had a flat nose, pointy eyes, and thick and fleshy lips. Ana had big round eyes, a sharp nose, and a beautifully drawn mouth and lips, but very thin. Whoever saw them would not guess that they were siblings, let alone twins! Curious was the fact that Ana looked more like Teresa than like her own brother. Teresa had, just like Ana, brown eyes, but even darker. Teresa was also short and thin, despite being slightly more curvaceous. Their noses were similar as well. She had a very pointy nose, although not long. What definitely distinguished them was the hair: Ana was a brunette, and her hair was straight and long. Teresa had bulky blonde hair, with lots of curls, which ended at her shoulders. Mário, Ana's boyfriend, was the tallest of all the people in the group. He was not fat but was slightly overweight. His arms and legs, just like his hands, were long. He wore glasses with such a thick lens that his eyes increased behind the lenses. His hair was black and seemed to be always unkempt. Rui, on the other hand, had silky brown hair. Rui was a bit vain, he always dressed well, and always looked good. He was very tanned, and his eyes were black, like an olive.

Entretanto, depois de a Ana e o Francisco terem chegado à estação, os amigos continuaram na galhofa até o comboio chegar, o que aconteceu não muito tempo depois. A viagem que iria demorar, de acordo com o previsto, 3 horas, era o início da aventura que tinha sido planeada ainda nos frios e longos meses de Inverno, por entre os corredores, salas de aula, e bibliotecas da Faculdade de Letras da Universidade de Lisboa. Na verdade, aquela ideia maluca tinha nascido vários meses antes, quando ainda faltava muito tempo para o Verão. Corria uma chuvosa e cinzenta terça-feira, no mês de Dezembro, quando o Rui viu no Facebook uma publicação do festival mais conhecido de Portugal—o Algarve Summer Fest—que iria decorrer no mês de Julho na bonita cidade de Tavira, no sul de Portugal. Eram apenas 8h53 da manhã, mas o seu cérebro pôs-se logo a pensar e o seu coração acelerou de imediato. Lembrou-se nesse instante dos seus amigos e fez o resto do caminho até à sala onde iria ter a primeira aula do dia a correr a galope. Assim que chegou ao anfiteatro, sentou-se ao pé dos seus amigos e logo lhes contou o que tinha visto.

Meanwhile, after Ana and Francisco arrived at the station, the friends continued joking around until the train arrived, which happened not long after. The journey that would take, according to the schedule, 3 hours, was the beginning of the adventure that had still been planned in the cold and long winter months, through the halls, classrooms, and libraries of the Faculty of Letters of the University of Lisbon. In fact, that crazy idea was born several months before, while the summer was still very far away. It was a gray and rainy Tuesday in December when Rui saw a Facebook post about the most popular festival in Portugal—the Algarve Summer

Fest—that would be held in July in the beautiful town of Tavira, in the south of Portugal. It was just 8:53 am, but his brain started thinking, and his heart sped up immediately. He thought of his friends right away and made the rest of the way to the classroom where he would have the first class of the day running at full speed. As soon as he arrived at the amphitheater, he sat by his friends and then told them about what he had just seen.

- Pessoal, vejam isto! – e mostrou-lhes o ecrã do telemóvel.
- Brutal, temos que ir! – disse o Francisco.
- Sim, sem dúvida. Já estou farta de estudar. Mas quando é? É que eu vou de férias com os meus pais em Agosto para o Norte, para a terra da minha mãe. – respondeu a Teresa.
- É em Julho, portanto não há problema. – disse-lhe o Rui.
- Então está combinado? Todos podem e todos vão? – perguntou logo Francisco, já muito entusiasmado.
- Sim! – gritaram todos em uníssono, pondo o resto da sua turma toda a olhar para eles, indignados com o barulho.
- Guys, check this out! – and showed them the cell phone's screen.
- Cool, we got to go! – Francisco said.
- Yes, without a doubt. I'm tired of studying. But when is it? I'm going on a vacation with my parents in August to the North, to my mother's hometown. – replied Teresa.
- It's in July, so there's no problem. – Rui told her.
- It's settled then? Everyone can go and everyone will go? – asked Francisco right away, already very excited.
- Yes! – they all yelled in unison, making the rest of the class stare at them, outraged by the noise.

Quando as aulas acabaram nesse dia, todos os elementos do grupo se dirigiram para casa com grande entusiasmo. Estavam desejosos de ir perguntar aos seus pais se estes os deixavam ir ao festival no Verão. E claro, se autorizariam, além da ida, o orçamento.... Afinal, os custos iriam ser elevados. Estas miniférias incluíam comprar a entrada para o festival, os bilhetes de ida e volta de comboio, dinheiro para a estadia, alimentação, um ou outro imprevisto, e claro, alguns *souvenirs*. Assim, na viagem para casa, cada um ia repetindo e ensaiando na sua cabeça aquilo que diria aos pais quando chegassem a casa. Pensavam em qual seria, enfim, a melhor forma de os convencerem. Além desta preocupação que os assolava, estavam também receosos por sabor o que diriam os pais dos amigos pois de nada valia terem autorização para ir se houvesse alguém do grupo a ficar de fora.

When classes ended that day, all the elements of the group headed home with great enthusiasm. They were eager to go ask their parents if they would let them go to the festival in the summer. And, of course, if they were allowed, in addition to going, the budget ... After all, the costs would be high. These mini-vacations included buying an entry to the festival, the train round-trip tickets, money for the stay, food, money for one or another unforeseen event, and, of course, some *souvenirs*. So, on the trip home, each one was repeating and rehearsing in their head what they would say to their parents when they got home. They were thinking about what the best way would be to convince them. In addition to this concern that worried them, they were also fearing what their friends' parents would say because it wouldn't matter if they could go if somebody on the group couldn't.

Ao chegar a casa, todos tentaram comportar-se da melhor forma possível. Punham as suas melhores maneiras, cara mais meiga e jeitos mais doces, para conseguirem levar os pais a proferir o tão ansiado "sim!". Nenhum deles foi corajoso ao ponto de fazer a pergunta ao chegar a casa. Todos esperaram a hora de jantar, para, em conversa amena e casual, lançarem a questão, como quem não quer a coisa. Apesar de terem esperado até à hora de comer para o fazer, não conseguiam deixar de pensar no assunto a cada segundo que passava. A Ana e o Francisco estavam particularmente nervosos, entreolhando-se constantemente. Foi então com grande entusiasmo e felicidade que mais tarde, ao trocarem mensagens no WhatsApp, puderam confirmar que os seus pais tinham acedido aos seus pedidos, e que assim, todos iriam, com certeza, passar juntos umas grandes férias, das quais, certamente, nunca mais se iriam esquecer!

When they got home, they all tried to behave in the best possible way. They prepared their best manners, sweetest face and softer ways, so they could lead their parents into uttering the much longed-for "yes!" None of them was brave enough to ask the question right when they got home. Everyone waited until dinner time, in warm and casual conversation to throw the question, like somebody who doesn't even care. Even though they waited until dinner time to do it, they could not help but think about it every second that passed. Ana and Francisco were particularly nervous, and they were looking at each other constantly. So it was with great excitement and happiness that later, when they exchanged messages on WhatsApp, they were able to confirm that their parents had accepted their requests, and so, they would certainly spend a great time together, of which they would never forget!

Questions

1) Where was the group of friends heading to?
2) Since when did the groups know each other?
3) Who found out about the event?
4) How did that person find out about the event?
5) Somebody had to check if they were free to go on a specific month. Who was it and which month would be a problem?
6) What worried the group when they were heading home after class?
7) Who in the group was particularly nervous?
8) How did the friends find out everyone else's parents had allowed them to go as well?

Answers

1)   To the Tavira, to attend the Algarve Summer Fest.
2) Since first grade.
3) Rui found out about it.

4) Through a Facebook post.

5) Teresa. She couldn't go in August because she would go on a vacation with her parents.

6) If their parents would not allow them to go.

7) The twins, Ana and Francisco.

8) Through a group chat in WhatsApp.

#2 – The First Day in Tavira

O grupo de amigos chegou à estação de comboios de Tavira ao final da manhã. A essa hora, todos eles estavam já esfomeados. A hora de almoço aproximava-se e a última vez que tinham comido tinha sido ao pequeno-almoço, várias horas antes. O entusiasmo da viagem tinha tapado as dores de estômago que a fome faz, mas agora que tinham chegado, não podiam deixar de as sentir. Assim que saíram do comboio, esperava-os um sol ainda mais quente do que aquele que os tinha deixado em Lisboa. Entusiasmadamente dirigiram-se à praça de táxis. A espera foi demorada, ou pelo menos assim lhes pareceu, já que estavam famintos. Ainda assim, de tão contentes que estavam, conseguiram ignorar o monstro que fazia barulhos esquisitos dentro dos estômagos deles.

The group of friends arrived at the Tavira's train station late in the morning. At that time, all of them were already hungry. The lunch hour was approaching and the last time they had eaten had been at breakfast, several hours before. The excitement of the trip had covered the stomachaches that hunger causes, but now that they had arrived, they couldn't stop feeling them. As soon as they got out of the train, awaiting them was a sun even hotter than the one that had left in them in Lisbon. Enthusiastically, they headed to the cabstand. The wait was a long one, or so it seemed to them, since they were really hungry. Nevertheless, they were so happy that they managed to ignore the monster that made weird noises inside their stomachs.

Já no táxi, e sem esconder a felicidade e o contentamento pelos dias de diversão que os esperavam, os amigos puderam ir vendo um pouco da maravilhosa cidade que os ia acolher durante praticamente uma semana. O céu sem nuvens deixava que o sol brilhasse claramente e iluminasse a paisagem. Viam-se alguns montes e planaltos, e bem lá ao fundo, filas infindáveis de laranjeiras e oliveiras. O verde seco, o laranja tijolo e alguns tons de castanho destacavam-se aos seus olhos. Eram as cores que dominavam o desenho que se lhes deparava. À medida que começaram a entrar numa zona mais urbana, mais residencial, começaram a ver casas pintadas a cal, muito tipicamente algarvias. Repararam também em alguns vestígios dos Mouros, que deixavam naquela terra, como em tantas outras, traços da sua identidade arquitectónica, mas não só. Felizmente, também alguns vestígios da sua língua perduraram na riquíssima língua Portuguesa. Em palavras como Algarve, Albufeira (que antes era Albuhera), Aljezur, Alfarroba, Alcácer do Sal, Almeirim, a influência é notória. O AL é um prefixo árabe—pelo menos foi o que aprenderam os amigos com o taxista que lhes ia ensinando um pouco da História do Sul da Península Ibérica. Assim, pensavam eles, já tinham algo interessante para contar aos pais quando voltassem.

In the cab, and without hiding the happiness and excitement due to the days of fun that were awaiting them, the friends were able to see a bit of the beautiful city that would receive them for almost a week. The cloudless sky let the sun shine clearly and illuminate the landscape. They could see some small hills and plateaus, and right there in the background, endless rows of orange and olive trees. Tones of dry green, brick orange and some shades of brown just jumped to their eyes. Those were the colors that dominated the painting that lay before them. As they began to get into a more urban, more residential area, they began to see houses painted with lime, very typical in the Algarve. They also noticed some traces of the Moors' heritage, who left, in that land, as so many others, traces of their architectural identity, but not only that. Fortunately, some traces of their idiom stuck to the rich Portuguese language. In words such as Algarve, Albufeira (formerly Albuhera), Aljezur, Alfarroba, Alcácer do Sal, Almeirim, the influence is notorious. AL is an

Arabic prefix—at least that's what the friends learned from the driver, who was teaching them a bit of the history of the South of the Iberian Peninsula. Well, so they thought, now they had something interesting to tell their parents when they got back.

O grupo de amigos, de tão excitado que ia, ia acenando aos residentes e vários turistas que com eles se iam cruzando. Estes, vagarosamente se turistas, apressadamente se residentes, seguiam as suas vidas, mas frequentemente acenavam de volta perante um grupo de jovens tão bem-disposto. Como a fome já não podia esperar mais, perguntaram ao taxista onde poderiam encontrar um bom restaurante perto do hotel, onde se comessem pratos típicos da cidade.

The group of friends were so excited that they were waving to the residents and to the several tourists they were coming across. These persons, walking slowly if tourists, quickly if residents, kept going on with their lives, but often waved back before such a cheerful group of young people. Since the hunger couldn't wait any longer, they asked the driver where they could find a good restaurant nearby to the hotel, where they could eat typical dishes of the city.

> - Podem ir ao 5 Mares. É mesmo ao pé do hotel. Basta descer as escadas para a praia e virarem à direita depois da esquina. Não há nada que enganar. É o meu restaurante favorito. Aconselhava-vos a cataplana de marisco. É de morrer e chorar por mais. Só de pensar que lhe sinto o sabor. – disse o taxista, olhando para o vazio, com a boca a salivar.
> - Muito obrigada, caro senhor! – agradeceu a Teresa.
> - Pode-nos dizer quanto tempo demoramos a pé? – perguntou ainda o Francisco.
> - Com certeza! Em menos de 10 minutos põem-se lá, sem dúvida. – respondeu o taxista, prontamente.
> - You can go to "5 Mares". It is right by the hotel. Just down the stairs to the beach and turn right around the corner. It's easy-peasy. It's my favorite restaurant. I advise you to order the shellfish *cataplana*. It is to die for. Just thinking about it

and I can taste it. – said the taxi driver, looking away, his mouth salivating.

- Thank you so much, dear sir! – thanked Teresa.

- Can you tell us how long it'll take us to walk there? – asked Francisco.

- For sure! In less than 10 minutes you're there, no doubt. – promptly replied the taxi driver.

Assim fez o grupo de amigos. Depois de fazerem o check-in no hotel, e deixarem as malas nos quartos, dirigiram-se para o restaurante, prontos a saborear o que de melhor a gastronomia algarvia tinha para oferecer. Saíram do hotel e seguiram o caminho indicado pelo taxista. Mas, das duas uma: ou o taxista lhes deu o caminho errado, ou eles enganaram-se porque o que acabou por acontecer foi que o grupo se perdeu e acabou à deriva pelas ruas de Tavira, que, naturalmente, não conheciam. Já tinham passado praticamente 20 minutos, e nem sinal do restaurante 5 Mares. Com dores de barriga por estarem cheios de fome, e dores de cabeça pela paciência que ia escasseando, o ambiente no grupo começou a ficar ligeiramente mais tenso. As gargalhadas e risos que ainda há pouco se ouviam tinham-se agora transformado em silêncio. Não seguiam exactamente ninguém—iam como que deambulando todos em grupo, com a esperança de encontrarem o restaurante por milagre. Até que o Mário, de todos o mais stressado, ansioso e com mau-feitio, perdeu o pouco de paciência que tinha e explodiu:

And so, they did. After checking in at the hotel, and leaving the bags in the rooms, they headed to the restaurant, ready to enjoy the best gastronomy Algarve had to offer. They left the hotel and followed the path indicated by the taxi driver. But either the cab driver gave them the wrong way, or they screwed up because what ended up happening was that the group got lost and ended up drifting through the streets of Tavira, which of course, they did not know. 20 minutes had nearly passed, and no sign of the restaurant 5 Mares. With tummy aches, because they were starving, and headaches due to the patience that was going to down the drain, the mood in the group started to become a little tenser. The laughter that was heard moments ago had now turned into silence. They weren't following anyone exactly—they were walking as a group, towards nowhere, but all with the hope of finding the restaurant as a miracle. Then Mário, of all the most stressful, anxious and bad-tempered, lost what little patience he had and exploded:

- Não aguento mais, tenho fome e estou cansado. Não percebo porque não entramos num táxi e lhe pedimos para nos levar até lá! – disse, quase em gritos.

- Mário, já te dissemos porquê! Estamos a trabalhar com um orçamento pequeno e modesto, caso não te lembres, e temos que tentar poupar ao máximo, até para podermos gastar naquilo que vale realmente a pena! – respondeu a Ana.

- Opá, não estejam para aí a stressar! Não se chateiem; que a gente há-de chegar lá. Mas também se não chegarmos lá nos próximos minutos sem problema nenhum—comemos no primeiro restaurante que nos aparecer à frente. O que acham da ideia? – tentou ajudar o Francisco. – Mal fora se nos fôssemos agora chatear por causa disto e estragar as férias?

- Sim, o Francisco tem razão. Não vale a pena perdermos a paciência por causa disto. Além disso, estamos com fome, o que não ajuda a discutir nem a pensar para descobrir o caminho. –acrescentou a Teresa.

- Tenho outra ideia: vamos para a praça de táxi e perguntamos lá as direcções a um deles. De certeza que ninguém nos vai negar essa ajuda, e assim também não gastamos dinheiro. Eu tenho visto várias placas que indicam que há uma praça naquela direcção. Não parece faltar muito, por isso eu acho que é a nossa melhor hipótese! Que me dizem? – propôs o Rui, animado.

- Sim, pode ser… – respondeu o Mário, meio contrariado e ainda com a cabeça a olhar para o chão.

- É uma boa ideia, vamos lá! – tentou motivar a Teresa.

- I can't take this anymore, I'm hungry and I'm tired. I don't understand why we don't get in a cab and ask to get us there. – he said, almost shouting.

- Mário, I already told you why! We are working with a small and modest budget, if you don't remember, and we have to try to save as much as possible, at least to be able to spend on what is really worth it! – replied Ana.

- Hey, don't stress about it! Don't get upset over this; we will get there. But even if we don't get there in the next few minutes, it's not a problem—we'll eat in the first restaurant that appears in front of us. What do you think of the idea? – Francisco tried to help. – How stupid would it be if we got mad because of it and ruined the holiday?

- Yes, Francisco is right. It's not worth losing our patience over this. Plus, we're hungry, which doesn't help when trying to discuss things or think. – added Teresa.

- I have another idea: let's go to the taxi square and ask directions to one of them. I'm sure nobody will deny us that help, and we don't have to spend any money. I have seen several signs that indicate that there is a square in that direction. Doesn't seem to be very far away, so I think it's our best chance. What do you say? – proposed Rui, cheerfully.

- Yes, we can do that ... – Mário replied, a little upset and still looking down.

- It's a good idea, let's go! – said Teresa, trying to motivate everyone else.

Já a caminho da praça de táxis, os ânimos não pareciam ter atenuado muito. O grupo continuava maioritariamente em silêncio, com a excepção do Francisco, que ora ia cantarolando, ora assobiando, ora dizendo umas piadas tontas para tentar animar o grupo e aliviar a situação, que se tinha tornado então um pouco constrangedora. A culpada era na verdade a fome, pois aquela má-disposição provoca o mau-feitio. No entanto, ninguém parecia ficar contagiado pela onda de bom humor que o Francisco tentava espalhar. A Teresa, por educação e simpatia, ia sorrindo sempre que Francisco tentava algo novo, mas não o fazia genuinamente. Até o Rui parecia completamente desmotivado e abatido pela falta de comida. Nem a ideia de que em breve iriam, possivelmente, encontrar as indicações para o restaurante mudavam alguma coisa. Na cabeça deles, à excepção, claro, do Francisco, iam chegar ao pé do taxista apenas para ouvirem ou que o taxista não sabia onde era o restaurante, ou que era muito longe, ou que estava fechado naquele dia. Imaginavam mil desfechos, e todos eles maus.

Already on the way to the taxi stand, the tension did not seem to have faded a bit. The group kept mostly silent, with the exception of Francisco, who was humming, whistling, or saying some silly jokes to try to cheer up the group and cool down the situation, which had become slightly awkward. The culprit was actually hunger, because that bad mood causes bad temper. However, no one seemed to be infected by the wave of good mood that Francisco was trying to spread. Teresa, politely and friendly, would smile whenever Francisco tried something new, but she would not do it genuinely. Rui looked completely demotivated and weary from the lack of food. Even the thought that soon they would, possibly, find directions to the restaurant changed anything. On their heads, with the exception, of course, of Francisco, they would talk to a taxi driver just to hear from him that he didn't know where the restaurant was, or that it was too far, or that it was closed that day. They imagined a thousand outcomes, and all of them bad.

Assim continuaram os amigos durante alguns minutos. Com a excepção, claro, do Francisco, cabisbaixos e calados, rumo ao seu "trágico" e inútil destino. Não fosse Francisco ser um rapaz que não se desmotiva facilmente, aquele dia teria, sem dúvida, acabado mal. Ao passar uma ruela apertada que iria levá-los à praça de táxis, o Francisco, que ia olhando distraidamente em seu redor, avistou um letreiro meio empoeirado que dizia algo que não conseguia distinguir claramente, mas que lhe parecia ser engraçado.

So, the friends continued walking for a few minutes. With the exception, of course, of Francisco, they were all sad and quiet, walking towards their "tragic" and useless destination. If Francisco wasn't a boy who hardly gets discouraged, that day would have, undoubtedly, ended badly. When passing a tight alley that would take them to the taxi stand, Francisco, who was looking around distractedly, spotted a slightly dusty sign that said something that he couldn't quite read, but which seemed to be funny.

> - Olhem o que diz ali: 5 Males! Devia ser o nome do nosso grupo neste momento específico—já que somos 5 e está tudo tão mal!... – disse o Francisco, que logo começa a rir sem parar.
> - Look what it says there: 5 Evils8! It should be the name of our group at this particular time—since we're 5 and everything is so bad! ... – said Francisco, who immediately started to laugh non-stop.

O Mário, que foi o único que olhou, embora quase por instinto, e que estava pronto para mandar o Francisco calar-se, por estar farto de o ouvir a ele e à sua boa-disposição, leu o que estava na placa.

Mário, who was the only one who looked, although almost by instinct, and who was ready to tell Francisco to shut up, because he was tired of hearing him and his good mood, read what was on the board.

> - Francisco, és um santo! Salvaste-nos! Mas és um santo tonto porque nem sequer te apercebeste do que acabaste de fazer, e quase íamos seguindo sem reparar nisto! É o restaurante! Não é 5 Males, mas sim *5 Mares*! – gritou o Mário, não cabendo em si de contente.
> - Francisco, you are a saint! You saved us! But you're a foolish saint because you don't even know what you just did, and we were almost going to keep on moving without

---

8 In Portuguese, the original name of the restaurant was "5 Mares" which means "5 Seas". When changing the "r" to "l", we've got "5 Males", which means "5 Evils".

noticing it! It's the restaurant! It's not 5 Evils, but 5 Seas instead! – shouted Mario, ecstatic.

O resto do grupo olhou imediatamente para cima e em direcção ao letreiro. Durante um segundo e meio, ficaram pasmados, sem perceber nada. A fome, mais uma vez, estava a atrasar-lhes a capacidade de raciocínio. Mas depois, os seus sorrisos foram-se formando, a sua tensão aliviando, o corpo relaxando... A energia, que parecia absolutamente esgotada ainda há instantes, voltou, inexplicavelmente, e logo se puseram todos aos saltos e a abraçar Francisco. Também a boa-disposição, que parecia só existir no Francisco, imediatamente contagiou todos, e a felicidade de estarem a começar uma grande aventura voltou. A fome, claro, ainda lá estava, mas foi esquecida durante uns minutos. O grupo começou então a dirigir-se para o restaurante, num ambiente livre de tensão, onde já só se ouviam gargalhadas e conversas animadas, sobre o que iriam escolher para comer. A verdade é que a fome aumentava à medida que sentiam os cheiros da gastronomia Algarvia a emanarem daquele sítio, mas sentiam-se tão contentes depois de tudo o que tinham passado, que já não sentiam essas dores. A paciência e a força estavam redobradas—e, por isso, ficaram eternamente agradecidos ao Francisco.

The rest of the group looked up and towards the sign. For a second and a half, they just stood still, without ever realizing what was going on. Hunger, once again, was keeping them from thinking. But then, their smiles started forming, their tension relieving, the body relaxing ... The energy, which seemed absolutely drained a few moments ago, came back, inexplicably, and soon, all were jumping up and down and hugging Francisco. Also, the good mood, which seemed to only exist in Francisco, immediately reached everyone, and the happiness of being at the start of a great adventure was back. The hunger, of course, was still there but was forgotten for a few minutes. The group then began heading for the restaurant, in a tension-free environment, and what could only be heard was laughter and joyful conversations about what they'd choose to eat. The truth is that hunger increased as the odor of the Algarve's gastronomy started to emanate from that place, but they felt so happy after what had just passed, that they no longer felt that pain. The patience and strength were redoubled—and, because of that, they were eternally grateful to Francisco.

Questions

1) In the first line of the story, a demonstrative pronoun is used. Which word is it?

2) In which tense is this verb conjugated "ficaram" (line 183)?

3) Grammatically, what is "nossa" (line 105)?

4) "Apressadamente" (line 44) is what grammatically? What would be the verb, noun, and adjective of the same word?

5) In the third line of the last paragraph, we can see the verbs "aliviar", "formar", and "relaxar" conjugated. In which tense?

6) "Francisco, és um santo!"(line 166) Rewrite this sentence in the future tense and in the past simple tense.

7) 5 Mares is the taxi driver's favorite restaurant. Which is the word that indicates that it is *his* favorite restaurant? How is that word referred to grammatically?

8) "Pode-nos dizer quanto tempo demoramos a pé?"(line 58) Can you identify a pronoun in this sentence? Of which type?

Answers

1) "Essa".

2) In the past simple tense, in the indicative form (In Portuguese, "pretérito perfeito, no modo indicativo").

3) A possessive pronoun.

4) Na – adverb of manner; Verb – Apressar; Noun – Pressa; Adjective – Apressado.

5) In the gerund.

6) Francisco, serás um santo. Francisco, foste um santo.

7) "meu" is a possessive determiner.

8) "nos" is a personal pronoun, more specifically, a direct object pronoun.

#3 – At the Algarve Summer Fest

- Não acredito que aqui estamos! – disse a Ana.

- É verdade. Sabe tão bem estar aqui com vocês, não é? – acrescentou a Teresa.

- A companhia não podia ser melhor! – disse o Rui. – São as minhas férias de sonho! E só agora começaram!

- O melhor ainda está para vir… – atirou o Francisco.

- Sabes que mais? Acho que tens razão! – concluiu o Mário.

- I can't believe we're here! – said Anna.

- It's true. It feels so good to be here with all of you, doesn't it? – added Teresa.

- And the company couldn't have been better! – said Rui. – These are my dream vacations! And they have just started!

- The best is yet to come... – said Francisco.

- You know what? I think you're right! – concluded Mario.

Todos estavam encantados com o pouco que tinham visto da cidade, do hotel, com o restaurante e a sua comida. Tudo o que tinham visto, provado, vivido, experimentado até agora tinha sido fantástico. Por isso mesmo, o Mário andava sempre com uma câmara fotográfica nas mãos, não fosse ele perder a chance de capturar algum momento único. No entanto, todos os momentos até agora lhe tinham parecido merecedores de captura, e então o Mário quase não falava com os amigos, tão focado que estava em arranjar os melhores ângulos para as suas fotografias.

Everyone was delighted with the little they had seen of the city, with the hotel, with the restaurant and its food. All that they had seen, tasted, lived, and experienced so far had been fantastic. Because of that, Mário was always with a camera in his hands, just so he wouldn't lose the chance of capturing a single moment. However, every moment until now had seemed worthy of capture, and so Mário almost didn't talk with his friends, so focused that he was on finding the best angles for his photos.

- Mário, tens que parar de tirar fotografias e aproveitar um bocadinho o que estamos a viver. Se estiveres só com a câmara a tirar fotos para depois relembrares estes momentos, não vais ter momentos para relembrar, e só os vais viver através do papel de fotografia... – disse-lhe a sua namorada.

- Depois do festival, até vários anos a seguir, todos me vão agradecer este esforço. Não vai haver nada melhor que estarem a ver fotos destes momentos tão especiais. E claro, para isso acontecer, há sempre alguém que tem que se sacrificar e andar sempre com a máquina fotográfica atrás! – respondeu-lhe o Mário.

- Eu não acho que seja bem assim, Mário! Nós até te podemos ficar gratos, mas tu vais ficar ressentido connosco porque o que vais levar daqui em termos de memórias vai ser muito pouco comparado connosco. Deixa isso e vive um bocadinho! Não é preciso tirar foto a absolutamente tudo... – disse a Teresa.

- Poxa! Vocês são chatos! Pronto, está bem, eu não tiro mais fotos... – cedeu o Mário por fim.

- Mário, you have to stop taking pictures and enjoy a little bit what we're living. If you're only with the camera taking pictures to remember these moments afterward, then you're not going to have any moments to remember, and you will live through the photographic paper only – his girlfriend told him.

- After the festival, and many years to come, everybody will thank me for this effort. There won't be anything better than being able to see the pictures of these special moments. And of course, for that to happen, there is always someone who has to sacrifice himself and be with the camera all the time. – answered Mário.

- I don't think it's quite like that, Mário! We can even be grateful, but you're going to hold a grudge against us because what are you going to take from here in terms of memories will be very small compared to us. Leave it be and live a little! There's no need to get absolutely everything on the camera... – said Teresa.

- Damn! You guys are annoying! Okay, I won't take any more pictures ... – said Mário, finally giving up.

O grupo já estava no recinto do festival. Absolutamente extasiados por estarem ali, e finalmente, que nem sabiam onde queriam ir primeiro. Este grupo de estudantes tinha esperado tanto tempo, ou pelo menos assim lhes tinha parecido, que agora que estavam mesmo lá, não conseguiam tomar nenhuma decisão. Ficaram ali todos especados, a olhar de fora para todo o frenesim de máquinas e infraestruturas montadas nas proximidades. Era algo realmente estrondoso e impactante. Decidiram ir para o fim da fila que os levava ao balcão da entrada, para que pudessem entrar dentro do recinto onde iam decorrer todas as actividades. Depois de ter passado pela entrada, onde validaram os seus bilhetes e lhe deram as pulseiras que teriam de usar durante todo o festival para poderem entrar e sair do recinto sem problemas, começaram a dirigir-se para o interior. Era cedo ainda – 3 da tarde – e ainda tinham muito tempo até ao primeiro concerto. No entanto, queriam ir entrando e adiantando as coisas, para não se atrasarem e correrem o risco de perder alguma coisa, fosse o que fosse. Além do mais, tinham que montar as tendas, e isso não se avizinhava ser uma tarefa fácil. Nenhum deles tinha alguma vez montado uma tenda, pelo que se mostravam um pouco preocupados.

The group was already on the festival grounds. Absolutely thrilled to be there, and finally, they didn't even know where they wanted to go first. This group of students had waited for so long, or at least that's what it seemed like, that now that they were there, they couldn't make a decision. They all stood there, staring at all the frenzy of the machines and facilities built nearby. It was something really stunning and impactful. They decided to go to the end of the line that led to the reception counter, so they could get inside the festival grounds, where all the activities were going to happen. After passing through the entrance, where they validated their tickets and were given the bracelets that they would have to use throughout the festival to be able to get in and out of the precinct without any problems, they headed inside. It was early still – 3 pm – so they had a lot of time until the first concert. However, they wanted to go in and start getting ahead of things, so they wouldn't be late and risk missing something, whatever it was. Besides, they had to set up tents, and it was a task that was going to be far from easy. None of them had ever pitched a tent, which was why they were a little worried.

Assim que começaram a caminhar pelo interior do recinto, perceberam logo que não ia ser uma tarefa nada fácil. O espaço, que até era bastante grande, estava cheio de gente já, e estava a ser difícil encontrar um sítio perfeito para poderem montar as suas tendas. Muita juventude já se tinha antecipado a eles, e ido mais cedo do que eles. Naturalmente, tinham escolhido os melhores lugares para eles, e já não havia muitas opções decentes. Apesar disso, o grupo não desanimou, e eventualmente, lá encontraram um espacinho até bastante agradável e plano, à sombra e à beira de um pequeno ribeiro, para poderem começar aquele próximo desafio. Tiraram as tendas das mochilas e puseram mãos à obra. Estacas voavam pelo ar, pedras serviam de martelos—a confusão reinava. Apesar de ninguém saber como montar tendas, ninguém teve a brilhante ideia de ler as instruções, até que a Teresa os lembrou disso. Escusado será dizer que até ao final do festival fizeram piadas com o facto de terem passado tanto tempo a montar uma tenda, para depois de lerem as instruções, o fazerem em 10 minutos.

As soon as they began walking through the grounds, they realized it wasn't going to be an easy task. The space, which was quite large, was already crowded, and it was hard to find a perfect place to set up their tents. A lot of young people had already anticipated them and arrived sooner than they had. Of course, they had chosen the best places for themselves, and there were no longer many decent options. Despite this, the group was not discouraged, and eventually, they found a spot that was quite nice and flat, in the shade and by a small stream, where they could start the next challenge. They took the tents out of their backpacks and started working. The tent spikes were flying through the air, stones served as hammers—confusion reigned. Although no one knew how to set up tents, no one had the bright idea to read the instructions, until Theresa reminded them of that. Needless to say, until the end of the festival, they all made jokes about the fact that they spent so much time trying to pitch a tent, to later, after reading the instructions, doing it in 10 minutes.

Umas horas, muito suor, e milhões de partículas de poeira levantadas, as tendas estavam montadas, e puderam sentar-se e descansar por uns momentos. Não quiseram, no entanto, perder muito tempo, pois queriam começar a divertir-se. Decidiram comer qualquer coisa para recuperar a energia e ir dar uma volta pelo recinto para ver que actividades e concertos iam haver naquela noite.

A couple of hours, a lot of sweat, and millions of dust particles later, the tents were assembled, and they were able to sit and rest for a while. They did not want to waste much time, however, because they wanted to start having fun. They decided to eat something to regain their energy and go for a walk around the grounds to see what activities and concerts were going to take place that night.

- Oh! Vai tocar o meu cantor favorito em menos de 15 minutos! Façam o que quiserem, mas em 5 minutos, eu vou começar a ir para lá! – avisou o Rui.
- Calma, Rui! A gente vai contigo! Como é que ele se chama mesmo? – perguntou o Francisco.
- Carlos Pompeu! É um grande poeta! – respondeu-lhe o Rui.
- Poeta? Então, mas isto não é um festival de música? Ou vimos para aqui ouvir recitais de poesia? – disse a Ana a brincar e a tentar provocar o Rui.
- Oh, Ana, usa os miolos! Ele não é um escritor, um poeta literalmente. Mas escreve letras lindíssimas, é liricista, autor, como lhe queiras chamar, e faz canções muito tocantes. Por isso, é nesse sentido que digo que é um grande poeta, que escreve grande poemas. – respondeu o Rui.

- Oh! My favorite singer is going to play in less than 15 minutes! Do what you want, but in 5 minutes, I'll start to go there! – warned Rui.

- Relax, Rui! We'll go with you! What's his name again? – asked Francisco.

- Carlos Pompeu. He's a great poet! – answered Rui.

- Poet? Isn't this a music festival? Or are we here to attend poetry recitals? – said Ana jokingly and trying to provoke Rui.

- Oh, Ana, use your brains! He's not a writer, a poet literally. But he writes beautiful lyrics, is a lyricist, author, whatever you want to call him, and makes very touching songs. So it is in that sense that I say that he is a great poet, who writes great poems. – replied Rui.

Todos conseguiram arranjar-se e ficar prontos dali a 5 minutos para irem ver o tão adorado cantor do Rui. Era apenas o primeiro concerto da noite, e planeavam assistir a todos, se a sua energia isso permitisse, independentemente de gostarem ou não. Por ser uma experiência que não queriam esquecer nunca, e pela incerteza de a voltarem a viver, não queriam desperdiçar nenhum momento nem faltar a nenhuma actividade. Queriam experimentar tudo e, num momento posterior, decidir e debater sobre aquilo que tinham gostado mais e menos. Mas, até ali, tudo lhes parecia igualmente perfeito, e único, inesquecível, memorável, inolvidável...

They were all able to get ready in 5 minutes to go see the beloved singer that Rui wanted to see. It was only the first concert of the night, and they planned to watch every single one of them, if their energy allowed it, regardless of whether they liked it or not. Due to it being an experience that they didn't want to ever forget, and also because of the uncertainty they would ever return, they didn't want to waste any time or miss any activity. They wanted to experience everything and, at a later moment, decide and discuss what they had enjoyed more and less. But, until that point, everything seemed perfect, and unique, unforgettable, memorable, indelible...

Questions

1) Write down the first three nouns that you find in the first paragraph that are feminine, and three in the second paragraph that are masculine.

2) What is the feminine form of the word "poet"?

3) Can you find, in the fourth paragraph, the first uniform noun (in Portuguese, "substantivo uniforme")?

4) What is the plural form of the word "papel"?

5) In the last line of the text you can find many adjectives together. What is their relation with each other?

6) On line 114, the word "literalmente" is used. What is that?

7) What would be the adjective equivalent to "literalmente"?

8) "Decidiram" is a word on line 102. In which tense is it?

9) Write down the previous verb in the infinitive form, and its adjective and noun equivalent.

Answers

1) Verdade; Companhia; Férias; Hotel, Restaurante, Momento.
2) Poetisa.
3) The noun "estudantes".
4) Papéis.
5) They are all synonyms of each other.
6) An adverb.
7) Literal.
8) Past tense.
9) Decidir. Adjective – decidido/a; Noun – decisão.

#4 – The Last Day

- Estou mortinho por dar um mergulho! – disse o Francisco.
- A quem o dizes… O sol queima como fogo! – concordou o Rui.
- Estás todo vermelho! Não puseste protector solar? És mesmo tonto! Eu tenho aqui se quiseres. – disse-lhe a Teresa.
- Ah! Não sabia que tinhas! – respondeu o Rui.
- Já tinha gritado para o mundo ouvir… Tu é que fizeste orelhas moucas[9]…. Queres ficar moreno, mas assim apanhaste um granda[10] escaldão… – disse a Teresa.
- Calmex[11], agora não vale a pena chorar sobre leite derramado… Eu sabia que tu me safavas; uma mulher prevenida vale por duas[12]. – atirou o Rui.
- Bem, tens razão. O que não tem remédio, remediado está. Vá, vem lá aqui para eu te por o creme nessas costas. Meu Deus…. Pareces uma lagosta ou um caranguejo. – disse ainda a Teresa.
- Opá e tu pareces uma lula, de tão branca que és. – provocou o Rui, a rir-se.
- I'm dying to dive in! – said Francisco.
- Tell me about it... The sun burns like fire! – agreed Rui.
- You're all red! You didn't put any sunscreen on? You are such a fool! I have it here if you want. – he told Teresa.
- Oh! I didn't know you had it! – answered Rui.
- I said that out loud for the world to hear ... You ignored it. You want to get a tan, but you just got yourself a sunburn... – said Teresa.
- Relax, now it's no use crying over spilled milk. And I knew you would save me; women are always prepared. – said Rui.

---

[9] "Mouco" means deaf. This expression literally means "making deaf ears", meaning, not hearing, intentionally, what someone said.
[10] It means "grande" (big). It is kind of like the logic between "a lot off" and "lotta".
[11] Slang for "Calma", which literally means "calm", and it has the intent of telling someone to calm down.
[12] Literally, "a prepared woman counts as two".

- Well, you're right. What has no solution, solved it is. Come on, come here so I can put the lotion on that back. My God ... You look like a lobster or a crab. – added Teresa.
- Hey, and you look like a squid, being as white as you are. – Rui provoked her, laughing.

Enquanto estes dois continuavam, distraidamente, à bulha, o Rui continuava ainda à procura do caminho para a praia. Iam andando e rindo, por todas as parvoíces que lhes saíam da boca. Poderia dizer-se que o Francisco, de todos o mais engraçado, ia particularmente inspirado:

While these two kept fighting distractedly, Rui was still looking for the right way to the beach. They were walking and laughing, due to all of the nonsense that was coming out of their mouths. It could be said that Francisco, the funniest of them all, was particularly inspired:

- Estavam duas cebolas numa panela a fumegar. E uma diz assim "Que calor!", e a outra vira-se e diz "Ha! Uma cebola que fala!" – diz ele, completamente às gargalhadas.
- Francisco, a sério, que piada tão seca! Ainda assim pões toda a gente à gargalhada! Tu és mesmo *de partir o coco a rir*![13] – disse, às gargalhadas, o Rui.
- Olha, se não nos concentrarmos, não vamos encontrar a praia. Eles devem estar preocupados! Ou então deliciados, por se livrarem de nós! – lembrou a Teresa.
- Bem, pelo que percebi do senhor da recepção, temos que subir aquela subida, depois virar à esquerda, em direcção a umas escadas, descê-las e já está. – disse Francisco, tentando ajudar.
- Pois, Francisco, complicado era descer uma subida... – brincou a Teresa.
- Oh, tu percebeste, oh chica esperta!

- There were two onions in a boiling pot. And one says, "It's so hot!", and the other turns around and says "Ha! An onion that speaks!" – he says, completely in stitches.
- Francisco, seriously, what a lame joke! Yet you make everyone laugh! You are really funny! –said Rui, laughing.
- Look, if we don't focus, we won't find the beach. They must be worried! Or maybe delighted, for getting rid of us! – Teresa recalled.
- Well, from what I understood at the reception desk, we have to go up that hill, then turn left towards the stairs, get down, and that's it. – said Francisco, trying to help.
- Right, Francisco, it would be complicated to go down a hill… – joked Teresa.
- Oh, you know what I meant, smartass!

Entretanto, já iam avistando a praia. Era a primeira vez que lá iam, e logo no último dia de férias em Tavira. Como tinham montado a tenda perto de um pequeno ribeiro, e as noites tinham sido bastante activas e desgastantes, os dias eram aproveitados para dormir e descansar. Não lhes apetecia ter que andar para a praia quando podiam refrescar-se logo ali naquele ribeiro. No entanto, não queriam ir embora de Tavira sem visitar as suas famosas praias. Decidiram, então, no último dia que tinham, visitar a praia de Tavira. Estavam, pois, muito animados e entusiasmados, e nem o facto de estarem absolutamente esgotados e de ser o último dia ali lhes retirava a alegria e a boa-disposição.

Meanwhile, they started seeing the beach. It was the first time they went there, and right on the last day of holiday in Tavira. Since they had their tent near a small stream, and the nights had been quite active and exhausting, the days were used for sleep and rest. They didn't feel like having to walk to the beach when they could take a dip right there on that stream. Nevertheless, they didn't want to leave Tavira without visiting its famous beaches. They then decided that on the last day they would visit the beach of Tavira. They were, therefore, very excited and enthusiastic, and not even the fact they were absolutely exhausted, plus being the last day that they were there, affected their joy and good mood.

Quando finalmente chegaram à praia, o Rui, o Francisco, ea Teresa depararam-se com a árdua missão de encontrar o resto do grupo—o Mário e aAna. Estes dois tinham-se levantado um pouco mais cedo que os outros para irem dar uma volta e namorar um pouco a sós. Mas agora queriam encontrar-se e não viam como o iriam fazer. A praia estava cheia de pessoas, e nem Mário nem Ana atendiam o telemóvel.

When they finally reached the beach, Rui, Francisco, and Teresa faced the arduous task of finding the rest of the group—Mário and Ana. These two had gotten up slightly earlier than the others to go for a walk and to have a little alone time together. But now they wanted to meet and didn't know how to. The beach was full of people, and neither Mário nor Ana answered their cell phones.

> - Devem ter ido dar um mergulho… – assumiu a Teresa.
> - Eu é que vou dar um mergulho, não tarda nada! – atirou o Francisco, a suar em bica.
> - Eu acho é que aqueles comilões estão no bar a petiscar! – supôs o Rui. – Vamos lá ver!
> - Maybe they went for a swim… – assumed Teresa.
> - I am the one who is going to take a dip, in no time! – said Francisco, sweating profusely.
> - I think those hungry gannets are in the bar, having a snack. – assumed Rui. – Let's see!

E assim fizeram. A caminho do bar, o Francisco não aguentou e correu a toda a velocidade para dar um mergulho, voltando logo de seguida. Nem 3 minutos demorou. E afinal, o Rui tinha razão e conhecia os seus amigos como ninguém. Lá sentados estavam o Mário e a Ana, a comer uma sandes de queijo cada um. Também os recém-chegados decidiram sentar-se a comer. Aprenderam da experiência do primeiro dia que estar com fome não é nada boa ideia. E aquela aventura de Verão, prestes a terminar, acabava como tinha começado—com os amigos a sentarem-se num restaurante algarvio, com um grande sorriso na cara.

And so they did. On the way to the bar, Francisco gave in to the heat and ran at full speed to take a dip, returning right away. It didn't even take 3 minutes. And after all, Rui was right all along, and he really knew his friends like nobody else. Sitting there were Mário and Ana, each eating a cheese sandwich. The newcomers decided to sit down and eat as well. They had learned from the experience of the first day that being hungry is not a good idea. And that summer adventure in Tavira, which was about to end, ended how it began—with the friends sitting in an Algarve's restaurant, with a big smile on their faces.

Questions

1) In the second line, what figure of speech is used by Rui?

2) Can you identify any Portuguese saying or proverb in the first paragraph? Write it down.

3) Francisco tells a joke to Teresa and Rui. What figure of speech is used in it?

4) Teresa makes fun of Francisco for saying something a bit stupid. What is it?

5) Why was the group separated?

6) Can you find out, given the context, what the expression "de partir o coco a rir" on line 35 means?

Answers

1) A simile.

2) Orelhas moucas; Não vale a pena chorar sobre leite derramado; O que não tem remédio, remediado está.

3) Personification of the onion.

4) For saying "subir a subida", which in Portuguese is a pleonasm/redundancy.

5) Because Ana and Mário went to the beach earlier to be together alone for a bit.

6) It means that someone or something is so funny that you can even perform a very challenging task, like cracking a coconut, and laugh while doing it.

Chapter 4 – Basic sentences

In this chapter, you will find a small list of the most current words and sentences that you may hear if you visit a Portuguese-speaking country, or that you may need if you try to speak Portuguese for the first time. Be aware that the following lists are intentionally short. Many important words are missing—some you'll see on the pocket dictionary, others you might have read in the short stories, some might be somewhere in the adverb chapter, and others you'll find out by yourself. You are not expected to learn Portuguese by memorizing a bunch of pre-established dialogues. Instead, our goal in these pages is just to give you the absolute fundamental sentences that every language book presents their reader for their first contact with the language, and which can aid you if you're in a hassle in a Portuguese speaking country. We expect, however, that by the end of this book, you'll manage to build some sentences by yourself with no need to revisit this section of the book.

Starting out

My name is Pedro. – O meu nome é Pedro.

My favorite color is… – A minha cor preferida é...

My father is a driver. – O meu pai é condutor/motorista.

My mother is very young. – A minhã mãe é muito nova.

I have three brothers and one sister. – Eu tenho três irmãos e uma irmã.

I'm 25 years old. – Eu tenho 25 anos.

I'm fine! – Estou bem!

Let's go! – Vamos!

No. – Não.

What is your name? – Qual é o seu nome?

When is it? – Quando é?

Why? – Porquê?

Yes. – Sim.

Greetings

Everything okay? – Está tudo bem?

Good afternoon! – Boa tarde!

Good evening! – Boa noite!

Good morning! – Bom dia!

Goodbye! – Adeus / Xau[14]!

Have a nice day – Tenha um bom dia!

Hello! – Olá!

Hi! – Oi!

How are you? – Como está?

How have you been doing – Como tem passado?

See you later! – Até logo!

See you soon. – Até já.

---

[14] "Xau" is a very informal way to say goodbye, so use it only when speaking in an informal situation.

Thank you for your help! – Obrigado/a[15] pela sua ajuda.

Very well! – Muito bem!

You're welcome! – De nada.

Out and about

Can you help me, please? – Pode ajudar-me, por favor?

Can you repeat, please? – Pode repetir, por favor?

Can you translate for me? – Pode traduzir para mim?

Could you speak more slowly, please? – Podia falar mais devagar, por favor?

Could you write that down, please? – Pode escrever isso, por favor?

Do you speak English? – Fala Inglês?

Excuse me. – Com licença/Desculpe.

How do I get to…? – Como chego a…?

How much does this cost? – Quanto custa?

I don't speak portuguese very well. – Eu não falo Português muito bem.

I don't understand. – Não percebo/entendo.

I need to use the bathroom. – Desculpe, preciso de usar a casa de banho.

I need some help. – Eu preciso de ajuda.

I only speak English. – Eu só falo Inglês.

I understand. – Eu percebo/entendo.

I'm lost. – Estou perdido/a.

I'm not from around here. – Eu não sou daqui.

---

[15] You should use "Obrigado" if you're a man, and "Obrigada" if you're a woman—it doesn't matter who you're talking to.

I'm very thankful! – Eu estou muito agradecido/a!

I'm here on vacation. – Estou cá de férias.

I'm sorry. – Lamento/Desculpe.

Just a moment. – Um momento.

Let's go! – Vamos!

Nice to meet you! – Prazer em conhecê-lo/a!

No problem. – Sem problema/Não há problema.

Please say that again. – Por favor diga isso mais uma vez.

Please. – Por favor.

Regards! – Cumprimentos!

See you later! – Até logo!

See you soon! – Até já!

See you tomorrow! – Até amanhã!

Sure. – Claro/Com certeza.

Thank you! – Obrigado/a!

What does that mean? – O que significa isso?

What time does this place open/close? – A que horas abre/fecha?

What time is it? – Que horas são?

Where does this train/bus go? – Para onde vai esse comboio/autocarro?

Where is the bathroom? – Onde é a casa de banho?

Helpful Lists

In this chapter, we have prepared a few different sets of lists that may be helpful on several occasions. Just browse through them and come back whenever you deem fit.

PT vs. BR Portuguese

A few different words

As we have said, the Portuguese spoken in Portugal differs a little from the Portuguese spoken in Brazil. With that in mind, we have prepared a short list of several words that you may come across and not recognize. The word will be in English first, then translated in PT Portuguese, and then finally, in BR Portuguese.

Bathroom – Casa de banho / Banheiro

Boy – Rapaz / Moleque

Breakfast - Pequeno-almoço / Café da manhã

Bus – Autocarro/ Ônibus

Candy – Rebuçado / Bala

Cell phone – Telemóvel / Celular

City Hall – Câmara municipal / Prefeitura

Cool – Fixe / Legal

Draught beer – Imperial / Chope

Driver's licence – Carta de condução / Carteira de motorista

Flight attendant – Hospedeira de bordo / Aeromoça

Fridge – Frigorífico / Geladeira

Give a ride – Dar boleia / Dar carona

Grass – Relva / Gramado

Hello? (Answering the phone) – Estou sim? / Alô?

Ice cream – Gelado / Sorvete

Identity card – Bilhete de identidade / Cédula de identidade

Issue – Assunto / Negócio

Juice – Sumo / Suco

Line – Fila / Bicha

Money – Dinheiro / Grana

Nap – Sesta / Cochilo

Okay – Ok / Valeu, Tá

Police station – Esquadra da polícia / Delegacia

Sport – Desporto / Esporte

Subtitles – Dobragem / Doblagem

Suit – Fato / Terno

Team – Equipa / Time

To drive – Conduzir / Dirigir

To Shower – Tomar banho / Tomar uma ducha

Toilet seat – Sanita / Vaso

Train – Comboio / Trem

Tram – Eléctrico / Bonde

Truck – Camião / Caminhão

Underpants – Cuecas / Calcinha

Watercolor – Aguarela / Aquarela

Weight room – Ginásio / Academia

Different wording

> **Placement of the reflexive pronouns**:

Regarding the placement of the reflexive pronouns, in European Portuguese, the pronoun always comes after the verb. In Brazilian Portuguese, the tendency is usually to place the pronoun before the verb. Take a look at these examples:

▪ My name is André. – (PT) Eu chamo-*me* André. (BR) Eu *me* chamo André.

- Do you feel better today? – (PT) Você sente-*se* melhor hoje? (BR) Você *se* sente melhor hoje?

However, bear in mind that in negative sentences, in both PT and BR Portuguese, the pronoun always comes before the verb, like in these examples:

- My name is not André. – Eu não me chamo André.
- You don't feel better today? – Você não se sente melhor hoje?

➤ **nfinitive vs. Gerund:**

To describe something that someone is doing at this very moment, Portuguese and Brazilians use different tenses. In Portugal, they use the compound tense "estar a" plus the infinitive of the verb, whereas in Brazil, they replaced it with "estar" plus the gerund of the verb. Just take a look at these examples for it to become clearer:

- They are studying at home. – (PT) Eles estão a estudar em casa. (BR) Eles estão estudando em casa.
- While I'm cooking, my husband is taking a shower. – (PT) Enquanto eu estou a cozinhar, o meu marido *está a tomar* banho. (BR) Enquanto *estou cozinhando*, meu marido *está tomando* banho.

Common mistakes

In this list, we have compiled the most common mistakes among beginners and intermediate speakers and wrote it down for you. Some of them might have to do with the spelling of a word, others with grammar and the structure of the sentence, and some might be regarding the pronunciation. You should check out this list to correct the mistakes you might be making, or to avoid them in the future.

Grammar mistakes

➢ "Conhecer" vs "Encontrar"

These two verbs often create some confusion among beginners. Below, you will find a small explanation of the meaning of each verb and some examples to help clarify it.

"Conhecer" can mean:

- to meet someone for the first time, e.g., "I first met him when I was at the park." – "Eu conheci-o quando estava no parque".
- to know something which someone is talking about, eg., "Ah, yes. I know that restaurant." – "Ah, sim. Eu conheço esse restaurante."
- to know a place to which you have been before, e.g., "I know Japan." – "Eu conheço o Japão."
- "Encontrar" can mean:
- to meet someone that you knew before, e.g., "I met him again yesterday in the park." – "Eu encontrei-o outra vez ontem no parque."
- to find something, e.g., "I found a coin on the floor." – "Eu encontrei uma moeda no chão."

➢ "Poder" vs. "Conseguir":

In the same way, people who are just now starting to learn the language may find it difficult to know the difference between "poder" and "conseguir". Take a look at the following examples:

"Poder" can mean:

- to be allowed to do something, e.g., "I can go out until 1 am." – "Eu posso sair até à uma da manhã."
- to have the possibility, e.g., "I can look after your dog." – "Eu posso cuidar do teu cão."
- "Conseguir" can mean:
- to have the capacity to do something, e.g., "I can jump really high." – "Eu consigo saltar muito alto."

Tip: Both "poder" and "conseguir" are sometimes used interchangeably, but in general they take on the roles described above. The idea that "poder" is something like "can", while "conseguir" is something like "to manage" or "being able to", may help you differentiate the verbs. For instance:

- Can you pass me the water? – Pode chegar-me a água? (in a situation where you're just asking for somebody to pass you the water)
- Do you manage/are you able to pass me the water? – Consegue chegar-me a água? (in a situation where you're asking if somebody is able to do it—if for instance, the water bottle is on a high shelf.)

Incorrect spelling

➤ "Por que"/ "Porquê"/ "Porque"

These words work like the "why/because" pair. "Por que" and "Porquê" (why) are used to ask questions (implicit or explicit) and "Porque" (because) is used for answers. Take a look at the following examples:

- For what reason is he not here yet? – Por que motivo é que ele ainda não está aqui?
- Everything is dark. Why? – Está tudo escuro. Porquê?
- Marcos didn't come to work because he was sick. – Marcos não foi trabalhar porque estava doente.

Tip: "Porque" can almost every time be replaced by the word "pois", e.g.:

- I didn't go to the party because I didn't want to. – Não fui à festa porque/pois não quis.

➤ "Mal"/ "Mau"

"Mal" can be an adverb or a noun, and it is the opposite of "well", which means "bem". "Mau" (bad/evil) is an adjective. It is the opposite of "good", which means "bom".

- That smells very bad. – Aquilo cheira muito mal.
- My father drives well. – O meu pai conduz bem.
- I always wake up in a good mood. – Acordo sempre de bom humor.
- The dictator was a bad man. – O ditador foi um homem mau.

➤ "Mas"/ "Mais"

"Mas", which means "but", is a conjunction used to suggest contrast and "mais" is an adverb that means "more" and is the opposite of "less". Therefore, "mas" indicates opposition and "mais" indicates quantity. This mistake might happen especially in the spoken variation of Brazilian Portuguese. The Brazilian accent adds an "i" when saying "mas", which makes it seem that they're saying "mas". Nevertheless, you should be able to understand which one is being used based on the context.

- More beer, please. – Mais cerveja, por favor.
- I want to travel, but I don't have any money. – Quero viajar, mas não tenho dinheiro nenhum.
- The more I speak to her, the more I fall in love. – Quanto mais eu converso com ela, mais me apaixono.
- Clara did her best, but she didn't get the job. – Clara deu o seu melhor, mas não conseguiu o emprego.

➤ "Haver"/ "Existir"

The verb "haver", which means "there is" in the sense "to exist", has no plural form. So we can say:

- There was only one person at the bar. – Só *havia* uma pessoa no bar.

But if we are referring to a larger quantity, the verb remains in the singular:

- There were 30 people at the meeting. – Havia 30 pessoas na reunião.

- There are many ways to say "I love you." – Há várias maneiras de dizer "eu amo-te".
- There will be changes in the system. – Haverá mudanças no sistema.

➤ "Obrigado"/ "Obrigada"

This one is simple, but still, many people can slip up sometimes. As explained above, in Portuguese, women say "obrigada" and men say "obrigado", regardless of whomever they are speaking to.

➤ "Meio-dia e meia" - right/ "Meio-dia e meio" - wrong

12h30 pm reads "meio dia e meia", not "meio dia e meio", like it is usually, but wrongly, said. It is "mei*a*" (half), in the feminine form since it is referring to "*meia hora*" (half an hour). Hour, in Portuguese, is a feminine word. Therefore, saying "meio-dia e meia" is the abbreviation of "meio dia e meia hora", which would literally translate to something like "half a day plus half an hour". The same goes for 12h30 am, which would be "meia noite e meia" (literally— half a night plus half an hour).

➤ "Descrição"/ "Discrição"

With very similar pronunciations and written forms, "descrição" and "discrição" have very distinct meanings. "Descrição" means "description", while "discrição" means "discretion". So it's very important not to mix the two. Take a look at these examples to help clarify it:

- I appreciate your discretion when dealing with the issue. – Agradeço a sua discrição ao lidar com o assunto.
- The cops asked the victim for a description of the robber. – Os polícias pediram à vítima uma descrição do assaltante.

Tip: Maybe you have noticed that just like in the English language, one word has an "e" and the other has an "i". If you don't confuse the English words, you may use that clue to identify when to use each word.

➤ "Sessão"/ "Secção"

Here we have another case of two words that are written similarly, sound very much alike, but that might create some confusion since their meanings are very different. "Sessão" with two 's' means "session", and "secção" with the 'cç' means "section". For instance:

- Silence! The session is about to begin. – Silêncio! A sessão vai começar!
- Ice cream is found in the frozen section of the supermarket. – O gelado encontra-se na secção de congelados do supermercado.

➤ "Aonde"/ "onde"

Though both "aonde" and "onde" mean "where" in English, the word "aonde" suggests that someone is going somewhere, carrying the idea of movement and displacement, whereas "onde" indicates the place where something or someone is, being related to permanence. Take a look at these examples:

- Do you know where my keys are? – Sabes onde estão as minhas chaves?
- Where are you going? – Aonde vais?

➤ "Trás"/ "traz"

There is no distinction between them in spoken language—they sound the same. Nevertheless, their meanings differ significantly. "Trás" is an adverb of place that means "back", while always being preceded by a preposition, while "traz" is the correspondent of the verb "to bring", in the third person singular. See how it applies in the examples below:

- Money doesn't bring happiness. – Dinheiro não traz felicidade.
- There is no point in looking back now. – Não adianta olhar para trás agora.

Tip: More than any trick, mnemonic or memory clue, the context will help you decipher which word is being used and with what meaning. When writing, if you're having a tough time figuring out how to spell it, try conjugating the verb.

False Cognates

False cognates, or false friends, are words and terms that may look, sound or be written in a very similar way in both languages, but that have very different meanings. To help you out with these tricky words and sneaky friends, we have compiled a list of the most usual or known false cognates you may find throughout your Portuguese journey. However, before that, here are a few tips to help you recognize some of the false friends that won't be featured on this list:

➤ Always check the meaning of new words:

Never assume that two words that sound similar in English and Portuguese have the same meaning. Look up the new words and write down their correct meaning;

➤ Learn false cognates with examples in context:

Context is extremely important when you are learning vocabulary! Never learn a word without an example of how it is used. Context always helps us understand what words mean. Take two words that sound very similar in English and Portuguese, find one sample sentence for each and you will quickly see the difference in usage between them;

➤ Practise with bad translations:

Have you ever watched an English film with subtitles in Portuguese? Try to follow them and pick out the mistakes! There will be more than you think. You can also try this exercise with translated texts.

- Acesso = Access || Assess = Avaliar
- Actualmente = Currently || Actually = Na verdade, na realidade
- Advertir = to warn or advise || Advertise = Publicitar

- Aluno = Student || Alumnus = Alumnus
- Amassar = To crush || Amass = Acumular
- Antena = Antenna || Anthem = Hino
- Aparelho = Equipment or apparatus || Apparel = Roupas
- Apontamento = Note || Appointment = Marcação
- Apreciação = Judgment, evaluation || Appreciation = Agradecimento, reconhecimento, gratidão
- Arma = Gun, weapon || Army = Exército
- Assistir = to watch (TV, for example) || Assist = Ajudar
- Assumir = to take over || Assume = Presumir
- Atender = Tend to, or to answer a call || Attend = Ir a, marcar presença
- Azar = Bad luck || Hazard = Risco, perigo
- Balcão = Counter (e.g. in a bar) || Balcony = Terraço
- Casualidade = Chance or coincidence || Casualty = Baixa, fatalidade
- Cigarro = Cigarette || Cigar = Charuto
- Colar = Necklace, or to glue || Collar = Colarinho, gola
- Colégio = Private School || College = Universidade, faculdade
- Compasso = Compasses || Compass = Bússola
- Compromisso = Commitment || Compromise = Entrar em acordo, fazer concessão, ceder
- Conceito = Concept || Conceit = Presunção
- Construir = To build || Construe = Interpretar
- Convicto = Convinced || Convict = Condenado
- Costume = Custom || Costume = Máscara, fato, fantasia
- Cota = Share, quota || Quote = Citar, citação
- Data = Date || Data = Dados
- Decepção = Disappointment || Deception = Fraude
- Dente = Tooth || Dent = Amassado
- Diversão = Fun || Diversion = Distracção, desvio
- Educado = Polite || Educated = Instruído, culto
- Esperto = Smart || Expert = Perito, especialista
- Esquisito = Strange || Exquisite = Belo, refinado

- Eventualmente = Possibly, maybe || Eventually = Finalmente, por fim
- Excitante = Arousing || Exciting = Empolgante
- Êxito = Success || Exit = Saída
- Fábrica = Factory || Fabric = tecido
- Físico = Physicist | |Physician = Médico clínico
- Gratuito = Gratuitous, free || Gratuity = Gorjeta
- Gripe = Flu || Grip = Agarrar
- Guitarra = Electric guitar || Guitar = Violão
- Hospício = Madhouse || Hospice = Abrigo para viajantes
- Ingenuidade = Naivety || Ingenuity = Creatividade, engenho
- Injúria = Insult || Injury = Lesão, ferida
- Jornal = Newspaper || Journal = Diário
- Lanche = Midday snack || Lunch = Almoço
- Largo = Broad, wide, or patio || Large = Grande
- Legenda = Subtitles || Legend = Lenda
- Leitura = Reading || Lecture = Conferência
- Livraria = Bookstore || Library = Biblioteca
- Maior = Bigger || Mayor = Prefeito
- Notícia = News || Notice = Observar, notar
- Ofício = Profession || Office = Escritório
- Parentes = Relatives || Parents = Pais
- Pasta = Folder, briefcase || Pasta = Massa
- Polícia = Police || Policy = Políticas
- Prejudicar = To harm, make damage || Prejudice = Preconceito
- Preservativo = Condom || Preservative = Conservante
- Pretender = Intend || Pretend = Fingir
- Próprio = Own || Proper = Adequado
- Puxar = Pull || Push = Empurrar
- Realizar = Accomplish, achieve || Realize = Perceber, dar-se conta
- Recipiente = Container || Recipient = Destinatário
- Recordar = to remember || Record = Gravação

- Resumir = Sum up, summarize || Resume = Recomeçar, retomar
- Retirar = Remove || Retire = Aposentar-se
- Rim = Kidney || Rim = Borda, beira
- Sapo = Toad || Sap = Seiva
- Sensato, ajuízado = Sensible || Sensitive = Sensível
- Suportar = to withstand || Support = Apoiar
- Taxa = Fee || Tax = Imposto

Terrível = Terrible || Terrific = ExcelenteNevertheless, there are also good cognates, true friends, on which we can rely on. If we follow a specific set of rules, there many words we can form directly from the English correspondent. For instance, the words that end in "ty" in English, transform to Portuguese easily, following one simple rule. The English suffix "ty" is equivalent to the Portuguese suffix "dade". So you just need to switch one for the other, while the rest of the word stays the same:

- Adversi-ty – adversi + dade = Adversidade
- Capacity = Capacidade
- City = Cidade
- Humanity = Humanidade
- Priority = Prioridade
- University = Universidade
- Velocity = Velocidade
- Simplicity = Simplicidade

With the words that end in "tion", we just need to switch it for "ção".

- Simplifica-tion = simplifica + ção = Simplificação
- Nation = Nação
- Observation = Observação
- Naturalization = Naturalização
- Sensatio = Sensação

For the adverbs of manner, which usually end in "lly", you just have to switch it for "mente".

- Natura-lly – natural + mente = Naturalmente
- Genetically = Geneticamente
- Orally = Oralmente
- Literally = Literalmente

In words that end with "ence", change that to "ência".

- Ess-ence – ess + ência = Essência
- Reverence = Reverência
- Frequence = Frequência
- Eloquence = Eloquência

Finally, or *finalmente*, many words that end in "al" in English are written the same way in Portuguese.

- Natural = Natural
- Total = Total
- General = General
- Fatal = Fatal
- Sensual = Sensual

There are, obviously, some exceptions, which don't exactly follow the rules. These set of rules work like a crutch—they are here to help you, but you're not supposed to rely on them all the time. To avoid making those types of mistakes, always double check what you're writing, and confirm the meaning and context.

Common idiomatic expressions, proverbs and sayings

Portuguese is a very old and rich language, so, naturally, it has its fair share of common expressions, proverbs, and sayings. In this list, we are going to focus on the most common or known expressions and proverbs that exist in the European Portuguese. Some of them might be applied and used in the other CPLP (Community of Portuguese Language Countries), with a slight or no variation, others might not be known at all—you can use them, though, and then brag about how you taught a native an expression he or she didn't know!

Also be aware that some expressions or proverbs have their translation, literal or not, in the English language. For those expressions that don't have one correspondent in the English language, its meaning will be explained.

'Bora! – Let's go! (Abreviation of the word embora, and used in situations where someone might say "vamos embora", but instead just says "bora")

A curiosidade matou o gato. – Curiosity killed the cat.

A dar com pau! – When there's a lot of something.

A esperança é a última a morrer. – Hope is the last thing to die.

A falar no diabo. – Speak of the devil.

À maneira. – It's great.

A mentira tem perna curta. – Literally, it means that a lie has short legs, meaning a lie can't go very far without being noticed.

A meu ver. – In my opinion, in my point of view.

À noite, todos os gatos são pardos. – All cats are gray during the dark.

À pala. – For free.

A pensar morreu um burro. – When somebody takes too long to make an easy decision, overthinking it.

A pensar na morte da bezerra. – To mope around.

A verdade é como o azeite, vem sempre ao de cima. – Truth, like oil, will in time rise to the surface.

Água mole em pedra dura, tanto bate até que fura. – Water dropping day by day wears the hardest rock away.

Aguenta os cavalos! – Hold your horses!

Amigos amigos, negócios à parte. – Friends friends, business aside.

Andar à nora. – When someone is not aware

Ao sabor da mare/vento! – To go with the flow.

Aqui há gato. – When somebody is sensing something is going on.

Armar um 31! – To create a chaotic situation, a fight, or a big problem.

Barata tonta! – A kind of aloof person that is confused and sloppy.

Burro velho não aprende línguas. – You can't teach an old dog new tricks.

Cão que ladra não morde. – Barking dogs never bite.

Cu de Judas. – In the middle of nowhere.

De boas intenções está o inferno cheio. – The road to hell is paved with good intentions.

Diz-me com quem andas e dir-te-ei quem és. – He who sleeps with dogs, gets up with fleas.

Em terra de cego, quem tem um olho é rei. – In the land of the blind, the one-eyed man is king.

Entre marido e mulher, não se mete a colher. – It means that no one should meddle in a couple's affairs or quarrels.

Estou com os azeites. – When somebody is in a bad mood.

Faço isto com uma perna às costas. – I can do this with my hands tied/in my sleep.

Fazer asneira. – Screw up.

Fazer de vela. – Being the third wheel.

Mais vai prevenir que remediar. – An ounce of prevention is worth a pound of cure.

Melhor tarde que nunca. – Better late than never.

Não adianta chorar sobre leite derramado. – It's no use crying over spilled milk.

Não é grande espingarda. – When something is not very good.

Não faço ideia. – I haven't got a clue.

Nem que a vaca tussa. – Not in a million years.

O gato comeu-lhe a língua. – When somebody doesn't say anything at all.

O pior cego é aquele que não quer ver. – There is no worse blind man than the one who doesn't want to see.

Por uma unha negra/por um triz. – By the skin of our teeth.

Pulga atrás da orelha. – When something is suspicious.

Quem anda à chuva molha-se. – It means that when you put yourself in certain situations, you'll have to deal with its consequences.

Quem me dera! – I wish!

Quem não arrisca, não petisca. – No pain, no gain.

Quem ri por último, ri melhor. – He who laughs last, laughs best.

Quem sai aos seus não degenera. – The apple doesn't fall far from the tree.

Só por cima do meu cadáver. – Over my dead body!

Tenho um olho no burro, o outro no cigano. –   Paying attention to everything that is going on around you.

Verdade nua e crua. – The whole, unvarnished truth.

Slang terms

We have decided to include a list of slang terms in this book as they are a big component of a language, especially for whoever wants to be fluent, to learn it fully and properly, and to then use it with natives. Additionally, it is something that is not usually thought of when teaching the language to foreigners, but it is something that is a part of the language, undoubtedly. And if the natives when they're young are exposed to all of the slang, foreigners are learning the language from a book or in a classroom, where formal speech is encouraged, and slang is often not appropriated at all. However, it would be impossible to understand the Portuguese spoken in Portugal in an every-day situation if you don't know the basic slang terms, which people use all the time, even at a café or restaurant. Plus, if you're starting a conversation with somebody new, it will always be a good thing to add some slang to your vocabulary—that will impress them for sure!À borla – For free

À toa – Someone doing something without putting much thought into it

Abananado – Shaken, confused

Abancar – To sit down

Afiambrar – Get close or hold of something that likely you were not supposed to.

Arrochar – Fall asleep

Até sabe a pato – Something that is really appreciated

Bacano – A cool dude

Banhada – To steal or to fool someone

Baril – Cool, nice

Bater a bota – Die

Bater couro – To woe, hit on someone

Beca – A little

Beijoca – Little kiss

Bezana – Being wasted

Bica – Expresso

Bimbo – A fool, hillbilly

Bué – A lot

Cadela – Being wasted

Cagar – Poo

Carcanhol – Money

Chavalo – Dude

Cochilo – Nap

Coiso/a – Thingy

Cortes – To bail out of something

Curtir – Make out with someone, or enjoy something

Dar bandeira – Draw attention

Dar barra – To deny something to someone, quite unexpectedly

Dar cana – Draw attention

Esticar o pernil – Die

Fino – Tap beer

Fixe – Cool, nice

Fogo! – Damn!

Ganda mel – Very nice, good

Gato/a – Hot dude or girl

Gregar – Vomit

Guita – Money

Jajão – Fail

Mão de vaca – Cheap person

Massa – Money

Meu – Dude, man

Mijar – Pee

Molhe – A lot

Na boa – It's cool

Narsa – Drunk, wasted

Nite – Cigarette

Papel – Money

Pasta – Money

Pilim – Money

Poça! – Damn!

Porrada – Beating

Puxa! – Yikes!

Tá-se bem – That's okay

Tipo – Like (something)

Tótil – A lot

Tranqui – Relax (short for "Tranquilo")

Um coche – A bit

Xoné – A fool, crazy person

Xôxo – Peck on the cheek

Ya – Yes

Pocket dictionary

We have prepared this small dictionary for you so that whenever you're in need of finding the translation or the correct spelling for a word you don't know or remember, you have the answer close by. This will obviously help you throughout the reading of this book, but also after you're done with it—if you ever feel you have to brush up on your vocabulary or just make sure the word you're looking for is the right one, this pocket dictionary will be a great tool. If, in any case, the word you are looking for is not in our dictionary, check out this high-quality and reliable online dictionary - **Cambridge Dictionary**.

A billion – Um bilião

A million – Um milhão

A thousand – Mil

Accelerator – Acelerador

Accident – Acidente

Achilles tendon – Tendão de Aquiles

Adam's apple – Maçã-de-adão

Agnostic – Agnótico

Alcoholic – Alcóolico

Anatomy – Anatomia

Anchovy – Anchova

Animals – Animais

Ankle – Tornozelo

Annual – Anual

Ant – Formiga

Anus – Ânus

Appendix – Apêndice

Apple – Maçã

Apple Tree – Macieira

April – Abril

April Fools – Dia das Mentiras

Arm – Braço

Armpit – Axila/Sovaco

Artery – Artéria

Atheist – Ateu/ateia

August – Agosto

Aunt – Tia

Automatic – Automático

Baby foods – Comida de bebé

Baby wipes – Toalhitas de bebé

Back – Costas

Back seat – Lugar de trás

Backbone – Coluna vertebral

Bag – Saco

Bagpack – Mochila

Balance – Saldo

Barley - Cevada

Batteries – Pilhas

Battery – Bateria

Bear – Urso

Beard – Barba

Bee – Abelha

Beef – Vaca

Beer – Cerveja

Belly – Barriga

Belly button – Umbigo

Belt – Cinto

Best friend – Melhor amigo/a

Beverages – Bebidas

Bicycle – Bicicleta

Big toe – Dedo grande

Bile – Bílis

Bird – Pássaro

Black – Preto

Bladder – Bexiga

Blinker – Piscas

Blood – Sangue

Blossom – Florescer

Blouse – Blusa

Blue – Azul

Boat – Barco

Bone – Osso

Books – Livros

Bottle – Garrafa

Bottom – Rabo

Bowl – Tigela

Boy – Rapaz/Menino

Boyfriend – Namorado

Brain – Cérebro

Brake light – Luz de travão

Branch – Ramo

Brassiere – Soutien

Bread counter – Padaria

Breasts – Seios

Breath – Hálito

Breathing – Respiração

Breeze – Brisa

Brother-in-law – Cunhado

Brown – Castanho

Buddhist – Budista

Bug – Bicho / Insecto

Bull – Touro

Bumper – Autocolante

Bush – Arbusto

Butter – Manteiga

Butterfly – Borboleta

Buttocks – Nádegas

Cable – Cabo

Cactus – Cacto

Calf (body part) – Gémeo

Camping – Acampar

Cancel – Cancelar

Candle – Vela

Car – Carro

Caravan – Caravana

Card – Cartão

Carnival – Carnaval

Cartilage – Cartilagem

Cat – Gato

Catholic – Católico

Century – Século

Cheap – Barato

Cheek – Bochecha

Cheese – Queijo

Cherry – Cereja

Cherry tree – Cerejeira

Chest – Peito

Chestnut tree – Castanheiro

Chicken – Galinha/Frango

Child – Criança

Child Seat – Cadeira de criança

Chin – Queixo

Chocolate – Chocolate

Christian – Cristão

Christmas – Natal

Christmas Eve – Consoada

Church – Igreja

Cider – Sidra

Clams – Amêijoas

Claw – Garra

Climate – Clima

Clock – Relógio

Clouds – Nuvens

Clutch – Embraiagem

Cock – Galo

Coconut - Coco

Codfish – Bacalhau

Coffee – Café

Cold – Frio

Collarbone/clavicle – Clavícula

Cologne – Colónia

Colors – Cores

Components - Componentes

Conditioner – Amaciador

Condoms – Preservativos

Convertible – Descapotável

Corn – Milho

Cornea – Córnea

Cotton – Algodão

Country – País

Cousin – Primo/a

Cow – Vaca

Crab – Caranguejo

Crow – Corvo

Cry – Choro

Cup – Chávena

Cutlery – Talheres

Cyclist – Ciclista

Dashboard – Tablier

Daughter – Filha

Daughter-in-law – Nora

Day after tomorrow – Depois de amanhã

Day before yesterday – Anteontem

Day off – Folga

Days of the week – Dias da semana

December – Dezembro

Deer – Veado

Defecate – Defecar

Degrees – Graus

Dental floss – Fio dental

Deodorant – Desodorizante

Desserts – Sobremesas

Diapers – Fraldas

Diesel – Gasóleo

Dog – cão

Door lock – Fechadura da porta

Dove – Pomba

Dress – Vestido

Drinks – Bebidas

Drive – Conduzir

Driver's seat – Lugar do condutor

Drought – Seca

Dry – Seco

Duck – Pato

Eagle – Águia

Ear – Orelha/Ouvido

Eardrum – Tímpano

Earlobe – Lóbulo da orelha

Easter – Páscoa

Egg – Ovo

Eight – Oito

Eight hundred – Oitocentos

Eighteen – Dezoito

Eighty – Oitenta

Elbow – Cotovelo

Elephant – Elefante

Eleven – Onze

Emergency – Emergência

Envelopes – Envelopes

Evacuate – Evacuar

Exhaust – Exaustor

Expensive – Caro

Eye – Olho

Eyeball – Globo ocular

Eyebrow – Sobrancelha

Eyelash – Pestana

Eyelid – Pálpebra

Face Powder – Pó de arroz

Fall – Outono

Family – Família

Fashion – Moda

Fat – Gordura

Father-in-law – Sogro

February – Fevereiro

Fiancé/e – Noivo/a

Fifteen – Quinze

Fifty – Cinquenta

Fig tree – Figueira

Finger – Dedos

Fingernail – Unha

Fire – Fogo

Firewood – Lenha

First aid kit – Kit primeiros Socorros

Fish – Peixe

Five – Cinco

Five hundred – Quinhentos

Flashlight – Lanterna

Flat tire – Pneu furado

Flesh – Carne

Flower – Flor

Fly – Mosca

Flies – Moscas

Fog – Nevoeiro

Food – Comida

Foot – Pé

Forearm – Antebraço

Forecast – Previsão

Forehead – Testa

Fork – Garfo

Forty – Quarenta

Foundation – Base

Four – Quarto

Four hundred – Quatrocentos

Fourteen – Catorze

Fox – Raposa

Freckles – Sardas

Freezing – Gelado

Friday – Sexta-feira

Friend – Amigo/a

Frog – Sapo

Front seat – Lugar da frente

Fruit tree – Árvore de fruto

Fruits – Frutas

Fuel – Combustível

Fuel tank – Depósito de combustível

Full – Cheio/a

Full beam lights – Máximos

Fur – Pêlo

Fuse – Fusível

Garage – Garage

Garlic – Alho

Gas – Gasolina/Gás

Gas pedal – Acelerador

Gentleman – Cavalheiro

Giraffe – Girafa

Girl – Rapariga/Menina

Girlfriend – Namorada

Gland – Glândula

Glass – Vidro/Copo

Glove compartment – Porta-luvas

Gloves – Luvas

Glue – Cola

Goat – Cabra

God – Deus

Goddaughter – Afilhada

Godfather – Padrinho

Godmother – Madrinha

Godson – Aflhado

Granddaughter – Neta

Grandfather – Avô

Grandmother – Avó

Grandparents – Avós

Grandson – Neto

Grapes – Uvas

Grass – Relva

Gray – Cinzento

Green – Verde

Groin – Virilha

Hair – Cabelo

Hairbrush – Escova de cabelo

Hairspray – Laca

Hake – Pescada

Halloween – Dia das Bruxas

Ham – Fiambre

Hand – Mão

Handbrake – Travão

Handkerchiefs – Lenços

Hat – Chapéu

Head – Cabeça

Headlights – Faróis

Headphones – Auscultadores

Headrest – Encosto

Hearing/sound – Audição

Heart – Coração

Heat – Calor

Heel – Calcanhar

Help – Ajuda/Socorro

Herb – Erva

Hiccup – Soluço

High – Alto/a

High heels – Sapatos Altos

Hip – Anca

Holiday – Feriado

Hoof – Casco

Horn – Buzina

Horse – Cavalo

Horse mackerel – Carapau

Hot – Quente

Humidity – Humidade

Hurricane - Furacão

Husband – Marido

Ice – Gelo

Ignition – Ignição

Indicators – Indicadores

Insurance – Seguro

Intestines – Intestino

Iris – Íris

Jack – Macaco

Jacket – Casaco

Jam – Compota

January – Janeiro

Jaw – Maxilar

Jelly – Gelatina

Jewish – Judeu

Joints – Articulações

Juice – Sumo

July – Julho

June – Junho

Kidneys – Rins

Knee – Joelho

Kneecap – Rótula

Knife – Faca

Knuckles – Nós dos dedos

Kyte – Papagaio

Lamb – Cordeiro

Lamp – Lamparina

Large intestine – Intestino grosso

Laxatives – Laxantes

Leaf – Folha

Leap year – Ano bissexto

Leather – Couro

Left – Esquerda

Leg – Perna

Lemon – Limão

Lemonade – Limonada

Light bulb – Lâmpada

Lighter – Isqueiro

Lightning – Trovões

Limb – Membro

Lime – Lima

Lion - Leão

Lip – Lábio

Lipstick – Baton

Liver – Fígado

Locker – Cadeado

Lost – Perdido/a

Low – Baixo/a

Lungs – Pulmões

Magazines – Revistas

Man – Homem

Manager – Gestor

March – Março

Mascara – Rímel

Matches – Fósforos

May – Maio

Meat – Carne

Meat section – Talho

Mechanic – Mecânico

Menstruation – Menstruação

Meteorology – Metereologia

Milk – Leite

Milkshake – Batido

Minibus - Miniautocarro

Mirror – Espelho

Moisturizing cream – Creme hidratante

Monday – Segunda-feira

Monkey – Macaco

Monthly – Mensal

Months – Meses

Moon – Lua

Moonlight – Luar

Mosque – Mesquita

Mosquitoes – Mosquitos

Moss – Musgo

Mother-in-law – Sogra

Motor – Motor

Motorbike – Motocicleta

Mountains – Montanhas

Mouse – Rato

Mustache – Bigode

Mouth – Boca

Mouthwash – Elixir Bocal

Mr. – Senhor

Mrs. – Senhora

Mucus – Muco

Muscle – Músculo

Mushroom – Cogumelo

Nail scissors – Corta-unhas

Napkin – Guardanapo

Neck – Pescoço

Needle – Agulha

Nephew – Sobrinho

Nerve – Nervo

Nervous system – Sistema nervoso

New Year's Eve – Véspera de Ano Novo

Newspaper – Jornal

Niece – Sobrinha

Nine – Nove

Nine hundred – Novecentos

Nineteen – Dezanove

Ninety – Noventa

Nipple – Mamilo

Nose – Nariz

Nostril – Narina

November – Novembro

Number plate – Matrícula

Numbers - Números

Nuts – Frutos Secos

Oat – Aveia

October – Outubro

Oesophagus – Esófago

Oil – Óleo

Ointment/pomade – Pomada

Olive oil – Azeite

Olive tree – Oliveira

Olives – Azeitonas

One – Um[16]

One hundred – Cem[17]16

Onion – Cebola

Orange – Cor-de-laranja

Orange – Laranja

Organ – Orgão

Outdoor – Exterior

Owl – Coruja

Painkillers – Analgésicos

Palm – Palma

Palm tree – Palmeira

Pancreas – Pâncreas

Pants – Calças

Paper – Papel

Passenger seat – Lugar do passageiro/pendura

Paw – Pata

Peanut butter – Manteiga de Amendoim

Peanuts – Amendoins

---

[16] Numbers one and two also have a feminine form when written before feminine nouns. So, "One boy – *um* menino" / "one girl – *uma* menina" and "Two boys – *dois* meninos / two girls – *duas* meninas".

[17] Every number over a hundred follows that same rule of the numbers over 20, but instead of saying "*cem* e um", it's said "*cento* e um", *cento* e dois", and so on.

Pear – Pêra

Pear tree – Pereira

Pee – Fazer xixi

Pelvis – Pélvis

Pen – Caneta

Pencil – Lápis

Pepper – Pimenta

Perfume – Perfume

Period – Período

Petal – Pétala

Phone charger – Carregador de Telemóvel

Photographs – Fotografias

Pig – Porco

Pigeon – Pombo

Pine tree - Pinheiro

Pineapple – Ananás

Pink – Cor-de-rosa

Piston – Pistão

Plants – Plantas

Plate – Prato

Plum tree – Pessegueiro

Pollen – Pólen

Poo – Fazer cocó

Pork – Porco

Pot – Panela

Pregnant – Grávida

Prescription – Prescrição

Pressure – Pressão

Protestant – Protestante

Pupil – Pupila

Purple – Roxo

Quit – Sair

Rabbit – Coelho

Radiator – Radiador

Rain – Chuva

Rainbow – Arco-íris

Rat - Ratazana

Rattlesnake – Cascavel

Razor – Lâmina/gillette

Razor clam – Lingueirão

Rear windscreen – Pára-brisas traseiro

Rearview mirror – Espelho retrovisor

Rectum – Recto

Red – Vermelho

Region – Região

Religion – Religião

Retina – Retina

Rib – Costela

Rib cage – Caixa Torácica

Right - Left

Road – Estrada

Roof – Tecto

Root – Raiz

Rope – Corda

Rose – Rosa

Safety pin – Pin de segurança

Saliva/spit – Saliva/cuspe

Salmon – Salmão

Salt – Sal

Sangria – Sangria

Sanitary pad – Penso higiénico

Sanitary towels – Toalhitas higiénicas

Sardine – Sardinha

Saturday – Sábado

Sausage – Salsicha

Scarf – Lenço

Scissors – Tesouras

Scooter – Scooter

Sea bass – Robalo

Sea bream – Dourada

Seahorse – Cavalo-marinho

Seasons – Estações

Seat belt – Cinto de segurança

Semen – Sémen

Semester – Semestre

Senses – Sentidos

September – Setembro

Serpent – Serpente

Serum – Soro

Seven – Sete

Seven hundred – Setecentos

Seventeen – Dezassete

Seventy – Setenta

Shampoo – Champô

Shark – Tubarão

Shaving cream – Creme de barbear

Shaving foam – Espuma de barbear

Shaving gel – Gel de barbear

Sheep – Ovelha

Shellfish – Marisco

Shin – Canela

Shock absorber – Pára-choques

Shoes – Sapatos / Calçado

Shorts – Calções

Shoulder – Ombro

Sight – Visão

Sister-in-law – Cunhada

Six – Seis

Six hundred – Seiscentos

Sixteen – Dezasseis

Sixty – Sessenta

Skeleton – Esqueleto

Skin – Pele

Skirt – Saia

Skull – Crânio

Sky – Céu

Skylight – Clarabóia

Sleeping bag – Saco-cama

Small intestine – Intestino delgado

Smell – Olfacto

Snake – Cobra

Sneakers – Sapatilhas / Ténis

Sneeze – Espirro

Snow – Neve

Snow tires – Pneus para a neve

Soap – Sabão

Socks – Meias

Soda – Refrigerante

Sole – Planta

Son – Filho

Son-in-law – Genro

Sour – Azedo

Souvenirs – Lembranças

Spare tire – Pneu sobresselente

Speedometer – Velocímetro

Spicy – Picante

Spider – Aranha

Spine – Espinha

Spleen – Baço

Spoon – Colher

Spring – Primavera

State – Estado

Steering wheel – Volante

Stepdaughter – Enteada

Stepfather – Padrasto

Stepmother – Madrasta

Stepson – Enteado

Stomach – Estômago

Storm – Tempestade

Strawberries – Morango

Straws – Palhinhas

Suit – Fato

Summer – Verão

Sun lotion – Protector solar

Sunday – Domingo

Sunglasses – Óculos de Sol

Sunny – Solarengo

Sweat – Suor

Sweet – Doce

Swimsuit – Fato de banho

Synagogue – Sinagoga

Table towel – Toalha de mesa

Tail – Cauda

Tampons – Tampões

Taste – Palato/paladar

Taxi – Táxi

Tea – Chá

Tears – Lágrimas

Teeth – Dentes

Temperature – Temperatura

Temple – Templo

Ten – Dez

Tendon – Tendão

Tent – Tenda

Testicles – Testículos

Thermometer – Termómetro

Thigh – Coxa

Thigh bone/femur – Fémur

Thirteen – Treze

Thirty – Trinta

Thorn – Espinho

Thousand – Mil

Three – Três

Three hundred – Trezentos

Throat – Garganta

Thumb – Polegar

Thunder – Trovoada

Thursday – Quinta-feira

Ticket office – Bilheteira

Tiger – Tigre

Tire – Pneu

Tissues – Lenços

Toe – Dedo do pé

Toenail – Unha do pé

Toilet paper – Papel higiénico

Tomorrow – Amanhã

Tongue – Língua

Tooth – Dente

Toothbrush – Escova de dentes

Toothpaste – Pasta de dentes

Tornado – Tornado

Touch – Tacto

Town – Cidade

Tractor – Tractor

Trailer – Atrelado

Tram – Elétrico

Tree – Árvore

Trimester – Trimestre

Trout – Truta

Truck – Camião

Trunk (car) – Bagageira

Trunk (elephant's) – Tromba

Trunk (tree) – Tronco

Tuesday – Terça-feira

Tuna – Atum

Turkey – Peru

Turquoise – Turquesa

Tweezers – Pinças

Twelve – Doze

Twenty – Vinte[18]

Twig – Galho

Two – Dois

Two hundred – Duzentos

Umbrella – Chapéu de chuva

Uncle – Tio

Underpants – Cuecas

Underwear – Roupa interior

Unleaded gas – Gasolina sem chumbo

Urgent – Urgente

Urinate – Urinar

Urine – Urina

Utensils – Utensílios

---

[18] After 20, every number in between 20 and 99, excluding 30, 40, 50, 60, 70, 80, 90 is the number itself plus and one, or and two, etc. So 21 would be "vinte *e um*", 31 would be "trinta *e dois»*", and so on.

Vagina – Vagina

Valentine's Day – Dia dos Namorados

Valve – Válvula

Van – Carrinha

Vegetables – Vegetais

Vein – Veia

Vertebra – Vértebra

View – Vista

Vinegar – Vinagre

Vitamin pills – Vitamínicos

Vomit – Vómito

Waist – Cintura

Warning light – Luz de aviso

Wasp – Vespa

Watch – Relógio

Water – Água

Wave – Onda

Weather – Tempo

Wednesday – Quarta-feira

Weekly – Semanal

Wheat – Trigo

Whelk – Búzios

Wife – Esposa

Wind – Vento

Window – Janela

Windpipe – Traqueia

Windscreen – Pára-brisas

Wine – Vinho

Wing – Asa

Winter – Inverno

Wolf – Lobo

Woman – Mulher

Womb – Útero

Wrinkles – Rugas

Wrist – Pulso

Wristwatch – Relógio de pulso

Yawn – Bocejar

Yellow – Amarelo

Yesterday – Ontem

Zero – Zero

Conclusion

Portuguese: How to Learn Portuguese Fast, Including Grammar, Short Stories, and Useful Phrases is aimed to give a basic understanding of the Portuguese language to beginners by laying out the fundamental grammar rules and overall structure of the language. However, its intent was not only to aid those who are just starting out on their trip into the rich world of the Portuguese language but also to continue guiding those who have already established and built a solid knowledge of the idiom. Having adopted both a non-communicative and a semi-communicative teaching method, this book first set out to give the basic tools needed to understand and speak the language. After that, a storytelling approach presented the reader with real-life situations and events, where they were encouraged to engage with the story, characters, and narrative, thus reducing the chances of demotivation, loss of interest, or boredom. Hopefully, this book served its purpose and was captivating enough to make you fall in love with the Portuguese language. It was paramount to offer a pleasant and exciting learning experience, which ultimately resulted in you being able to understand and express yourself in Portuguese.

Lastly—and this cannot be stressed enough—keep practicing your Portuguese! Learning a language requires a lot of studying and hard work. So do not throw away all the hours that you have spent taking these first steps. It is recommended that you revisit this book whenever you feel like you have to brush up on your vocabulary or grammar. Do not forget that as you advance to more demanding linguistic challenges, the knowledge learned here, as basic as it may appear, at first sight, is absolutely crucial when it comes to mastering the Portuguese language. Here is some final advice on what you can do to practice your skills:

- Read books! Either other learning books, or novels (always with your dictionary at hand);

- Practice your writing skills – try to write your shopping list in Portuguese, for example;

- Watch Portuguese movies – with subtitles in your original language, and as you develop your skills, with Portuguese subtitles;

- Hear music – check out the lyrics, and search for the words you are not familiar with and sing! (Music will also help with the correct pronunciation and accent);

- Visit Portuguese-speaking countries – there is no better way to learn than being completely immersed in the language, surrounded by real-life situations, and interacting with natives.

Certainly, your tenacity and perseverance will be rewarded at the end.

Part 2: Portuguese Short Stories

11 Simple Stories for Beginners Who Want to Learn Portuguese in Less Time While Also Having Fun

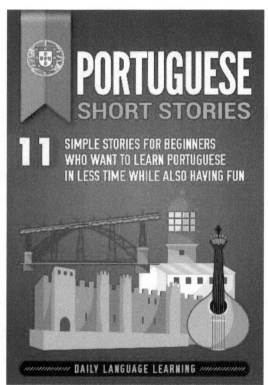

Introduction

Learning Portuguese is a tough challenge, no doubt about it. The rich vocabulary and complex grammar can be discouraging when you are taking your first steps into the learning process. The goal of this book is to teach Portuguese in the most effective way possible. It adopts a semi-communicative method—the storytelling approach. Telling stories is an effective educational tool because learners become engaged with the narrative and therefore remember the story effortlessly, the vocabulary associated with it, as well as making it easier to recognize sentence patterns.

However, "what more can storytelling offer?" Well, it brings you closer to how the language is spoken on an informal, day-to-day basis, instead of trying to teach how to form a sentence from scratch. When first starting out, and with no previous contact with the language, it is assumed that learners do not have much vocabulary, don't know how the grammar and/or syntax works, and have no clue on how to pronounce the words; thus, making it harder to emulate the teaching process of a language with which someone is familiar with, even if he/she doesn't know how it works formally. For instance, when you first started studying your native language in school, you had already heard its sounds by then—after all, you knew how to speak appropriately long before you started studying it formally. Even if intuitively, and with some mistakes in the middle, you knew how to build a sentence. So, with that in mind, this book aims, with this approach and in parallel to the experience of a first contact with your native language, to give you an intuitive feel on how to build sentences, aside from establishing the basic knowledge on grammar and wording, as well as teaching key vocabulary.

This being said, just before you start, take a look at the following set of guidelines that will help you navigate smoothly through the book. Some ideas and tips to help you after you finish the stories are also provided—most of them regarding ways to keep practicing your Portuguese.

A few guidelines...

This book comprises eleven short stories, one summary, and one vocabulary list after each story, plus a small quiz to test your overall comprehension of the text and the specific programmatic goal of the story. For instance, some stories and their respective quizzes might be more focused on the names of objects or verb tenses, and so on. Every story, summary, highlighted vocabulary, and quiz is also translated into English.

It is advisable to read the whole story twice before attempting the quiz. Underline every word you don't recognize and check if their meanings are written down on the vocabulary list. If not, check a dictionary. Do not just translate it to what you think it might be—since many words have more than one meaning, depending on their context. Thus, it would be useful to see the word used in a sentence—to do that, you just have to search the unknown word in the dictionary mentioned below, and it will give a few different examples of how the word is used in sentences. Another thing to help is writing down any commentaries or notes that you might find useful later on, on a third or fourth read, or when solving the quiz. And remember: try to do it in Portuguese if you can.

Additionally, read the whole story, summary, and quiz, first in the Portuguese version, and then try to sum it up yourself in English. If it becomes impossible to keep going without some help, go and check the English summary. If that doesn't do it, then try the specific paragraph, the one in English now. Then, finally, if these steps didn't help at all, read the whole story, every paragraph, in the English version. The stories, and the respective quizzes, are supposed to be engaging and moderately easy to follow, while always maintaining a degree of difficulty that is challenging, but never discouraging. So, even if you are not sure of what a word means in a specific context, if it is not in the vocabulary list, or your doubtful of what an answer might be in the quiz—don't give up right away. Try to do it all in Portuguese, and then check the answers—always after, never before.

Finally, and most importantly, practice Portuguese wherever and whenever you can. Speak to yourself in Portuguese, name objects around you in Portuguese, think in Portuguese, watch Portuguese movies, listen to Portuguese music, and visit a Portuguese speaking country! Whatever tools that will help you with the learning process are very much welcomed.

One last thing—there are many Portuguese speaking countries in the world. However, the structure of the Portuguese language was not unified until recently. There were, and still are, some variations and small differences in wording, spelling, and pronunciation depending on which Portuguese country you choose. The Orthographic Agreement of 1990 has changed the spelling of many words and made the written PT Portuguese much more similar to the spoken BR Portuguese. Even though the agreement is from 1990, it was only applied in Portugal in 2010. Nevertheless, since its use causes some controversy amongst some authors or writers, many choose not to write according to the agreement. Hence, this book follows the spelling of the previous agreement—before 1990. Don't worry if you see some words spelled differently in a newspaper or book—if it looks unfamiliar, just double-check—as most online dictionaries[17] have both agreements that are equally accepted.

Good luck or... Boa sorte!

---

17 Here is a good Portuguese dictionary - https://dicionario.priberam.org/. You can choose to use the spelling *pre-* or *post-*agreement.

Chapter 1 – O Primeiro Adeus

As **primas** Sofia, Sara, e Ana estavam aos **pulos** de tão contentes. Era a primeira vez que iam dormir sem os **pais** estarem por perto. Quando eram mais **pequenas**, tinham, por várias vezes dormido na casa umas das outras, mas era sempre quando os pais lá iam visitar os **tios**. Elas eram todas muito apegadas aos pais, e embora gostassem muito de estar **juntas** e de se divertirem, tinham um bocado de medo de passar a noite sem saber que os pais estariam por perto para qualquer coisa que eventualmente precisassem. No entanto, todas tinham já catorze anos, e os pais acharam que estava na altura de passarem por essa experiência. Os pais não queriam que as suas filhas se adaptassem mal quando tivessem que sair de casa para ir para a **faculdade**, e, além disso, também precisavam de algum tempo para si próprios.

Cousins Sofia, Sara, and Ana were so happy they were jumping up and down. It was the first time they were going to sleep without their parents being around. When they were little, they had, for several times, slept in each other's homes, but it was always when their parents were visiting their uncles. They were all very attached to their parents, and although they enjoyed being together and having fun, they were bit afraid to spend the night not knowing that their parents would be around for anything they eventually needed. However, they were all fourteen years old now, and the parents thought it was time for them to go through that experience. The parents didn't want their daughters to have a hard time when they had to leave home to go to college, and, besides that, they also needed some time for themselves.

Foi então com muita felicidade que as três primas ouviram a proposta dos pais delas. Estes tinham comprado uma **tenda** e três **sacos-cama** para elas irem **acampar** sozinhas um fim-de-semana. O parque de campismo era perto de onde elas viviam; de qualquer forma, iriam passar a noite sem os pais, iriam ter que cozinhar e, basicamente, sobreviver dois dias sem **adultos** por perto para as controlar. Naturalmente, levariam os telemóveis consigo; a **recepção** do parque de campismo tinha sido avisada para que se alguma coisa acontecesse, ligar logo ao pai de Sofia, mas a verdade, é que estavam por conta delas.

So, it was with great pleasure that the three cousins listened to their parents' proposal. They had bought a tent and three sleeping bags for them to go camping alone for a weekend. The campsite was close to where they lived; they would, however, spend the night without their parents, they would have to cook and basically survive two days without adults around to control them. Of course, they would take the phones with them; the campsite reception had been warned that if anything happened, to call Sofia's father immediately, but the truth is that they were on their own.

Na **sexta-feira**, as três primas já estavam super impacientes, e já só queriam ir para o parque, montar a tenda, e começar a sua aventura. Trocavam mensagens entre elas, combinando já mil e um planos e **brincadeiras**. Combinavam o que iam levar, o que iam vestir, o que iam comer... Mas, apesar de toda esta **euforia**, todas estavam um pouco nervosas. Tudo aquilo que as fazia sentir entusiasmadas também as assustava. E se alguma coisa corresse mal? E se não conseguissem sequer montar a tenda? Ou se tivessem medo durante a noite? E se não conseguissem cozinhar e ficassem cheias de fome? Ou, o pior de tudo, se tivessem que ligar aos pais para as irem buscar, o que iriam eles dizer? Será que iriam ficar **desapontados**?

On Friday, the three cousins were already super impatient, and they just wanted to go to the campsite, assemble the tent, and start their adventure. They were exchanging messages between them, making one thousand and one plans and jokes. They talked about what they were going to take, what they were going to wear, what they were going to eat... But despite all of this euphoria, they were all a little nervous. Everything that made them feel enthusiastic also frightened them. What if something went wrong? What if they couldn't even assemble the tent? Or if they were afraid during the night? What if they couldn't cook and got hungry? Or, worst of all, what if they had to call their parents to pick them up, what would they say? Would they be disappointed?

Estes pensamentos corriam nas suas **cabeças**, mas elas não os partilhavam entre si. Quando chegou a hora de ir, a ansiedade atingiu o seu pico, e as primas, a caminho do parque de campismo, nem falavam; já só mostravam um sorriso nervosa.

These thoughts ran through their heads, but they did not share them with each other. When the time to go came, the anxiety reached its peak, and the cousins, on their way to the campsite, didn't even speak; they had only a nervous smile on their faces.

Quando chegou a hora da **despedida**, até as barrigas começaram a doer. Despediram-se do pai de Sara, que as tinha ido levar e entraram, no parque de campismo para começar a montar a tenda.

When it was time to say goodbye, even their bellies began hurting. They said goodbye to Sara's dad, who had taken them there, and after, they entered the campsite to begin assembling the tent.

– Pronto, adeus! **Portem-se** bem, tenham **juízo**! – disse o pai de Sara.

– Adeus pai! – disse a filha.

– Até **domingo**, tio! – disse Ana.

– Se sobrevivermos até lá! – disse Sara, a sorrir.

– Okay, bye! Behave yourselves! – said Sara's dad.

– Goobye, Dad! – said the daughter.

– See you on Sunday, Uncle! – said Ana.

– If we survive until then! – said Sara, smiling.

Ao ir-se embora, o pai de Sara ficou com a sensação de que aquele iria ser um óptimo fim-de-semana, para elas e para eles. As três primas começaram a montar a tenda, e no início, tiveram algumas dificuldades, mas depois de seguirem as **instruções**, conseguiram fazê-lo. **Arrumaram** as suas **mochilas** lá dentro, e já estavam a ficar com alguma fome, então pegaram na **panela** que tinham trazido e começaram a tentar cozinhar qualquer coisa. Também a primeira **tentativa** de cozinhar não saiu nada bem, mas não desistiram, já que a fome não deixava. No fim, acabaram por comer um jantar um pouco queimado, que lhes soube muito mal! Ficaram ainda com tanta fome depois daquele jantar falhado, que nem fizeram nada do que tinham combinado depois de jantar, e foram logo para a tenda dormir. Só que nem dormir conseguiam, já que os mosquitos só as estavam a chatear bastante.

While leaving, Sara's father got the feeling that it was going to be a great weekend for the daughters and for the parents. The three cousins began assembling the tent, and at first, they had some trouble, but after they followed the instructions, they succeeded. They put their backpacks in there, and they were getting a little hungry, so they took out the pot they brought with them and started trying to cook something. The first attempt at cooking also did not go too well, but they didn't give up, since hunger didn't let them do that. In the end, they ended up having to eat food that was a little burnt, which tasted awful! They were still very hungry after that failed dinner, so they didn't do anything they had planned to do after it, and they went straight to the tent to sleep. But, they couldn't sleep as well, since the mosquitoes were bothering them a lot.

Entretanto, os pais das três primas estavam a divertir-se muito. Os três casais tinham ido jantar fora, e embora de vez em quando pensassem nas filhas e se tudo estaria a correr bem, sabiam que se se tivesse passado alguma coisa, elas tinham ligado, e nem sequer falaram sobre elas ao jantar.

Meanwhile, the parents of the three cousins were having a lot of fun. The three couples had gone out to dinner, and though once in a while they thought about their daughters and if everything was going well, they knew that if something had happened, they would have called, and they didn't even talk about them at dinner.

No dia seguinte, quando as primas se levantaram e foram fazer o pequeno-almoço, as coisas já correram bastante melhor. A experiência da noite anterior preparou-as bem, e conseguiram cozinhar um pequeno-almoço muito **saboroso**. Isso deu-lhes logo **motivação** e força para o resto do dia. Passaram a manhã a passear, e depois de almoço, foram para a praia. Tinham combinado ligar aos pais no **sábado** à tarde, para lhes dizer se estava tudo bem, mas estavam-se a divertir tanto que não se lembraram. Quando voltaram ao parque de campismo, tinham imensos planos de jogos para fazer durante a noite. Como era a última antes de voltarem a casa na manhã seguinte, queriam aproveitar todas as horas que conseguissem.

The following day, when the cousins got up and started to cook breakfast, things went a lot better. The experience of the previous night prepared them well, and they managed to cook a very tasty breakfast. That gave them motivation and strength for the rest of the day. They spent the morning taking walks, and after lunch, they went to the beach. They had planned to call their parents on Saturday afternoon to tell them if everything was okay, but they were having so much fun that they didn't even remember. When they returned to the campsite, they had a lot of game plans to play throughout the night. Since it was the last one before returning home the next morning, they wanted to enjoy every hour they could.

Enquanto o jantar na noite anterior tinha sido espectacular, o dia de sábado não estava a correr assim tão bem para os pais. Cada casal tinha a casa só para si, e o que no início lhes pareceu romântico, começava agora a ser estranho. Não estavam nada habituados a uma casa sem confusão e sem barulho, e começavam a sentir saudades das suas filhas e sobrinhas a correr de um lado para o outro. Nessa noite ao jantar, onde se juntaram na casa dos pais de Ana, já só falavam delas.

While the dinner on the night before had been spectacular, Saturday was not going so well for the parents. Each couple had the house all to themselves, which at first seemed romantic, but now began to feel strange. They were not accustomed to a house without confusion and without noise, and they began missing their daughters and nieces running around from one side to the other. That night at dinner, where they all got together at Ana's parents' house, they just talked about their daughters.

Quando a hora de as ir buscar chegou, eram os pais que estavam ansiosos. Tão ansiosos quanto as filhas na sexta-feira antes de ir acampar pela primeira vez. Estavam mortos por vê-las outra vez! Já as filhas estavam tristes por terem que ir embora. O fim-de-semana tinha sido **estupendo**. No início tinha sentido a falta dos pais, mas depois de se terem **habituado**, já não queriam outra coisa. Afinal, o que os pais achavam que ia ser uma experiência importante para as filhas, acabou por ser também uma valiosa lição para os pais!

When the time to get them came, it was the parents who were anxious. As anxious as the daughters were on Friday before going camping for the first time. They were dying to see them again! The daughters, however, were sad they had to leave. The weekend had been terrific. At first, they missed their parents, but after they got used to it, they didn't want anything else. In the end, what the parents thought was going to be an important experience for their daughters, turned out to be a valuable lesson for them as well!

Sumário

Sofia, Sara, e Ana são primas que vão acampar juntas pela primeira vez. Embora já tenham todas catorze anos, é também a primeira vez que dormem longe dos pais. Em crianças, dormiam sempre nas casas umas das outras, mas só quando os pais visitavam os tios. E nunca tinham ido dormir a casa dos seus amigos, porque, ainda que lhes custasse admitir, tinham um bocadinho de medo de se separar dos pais. Foram estes que tiveram esta ideia, já que queriam que elas tivessem esta experiência – algo que os pais consideravam muito importante. Mas no fim, a experiência acabou por correr bem de mais, e afinal, pôs à prova não as filhas, mas os pais!

Summary

Sofia, Sara, and Ana are cousins that are going to camp together for the first time. Even though they all are fourteen years old, it is also the first time that they are going to sleep away from their parents. As children, they would always sleep in each other's houses, but only when their parents were visiting their uncles. And they never had slept in their friends' houses because, even though it was hard to admit, they were a bit frightened to separate from their parents. It was them that had this idea, since they wanted their daughters to have this experience—something that the parents thought was very important. But when it was all said and done, the experience ended up going too well, and in the end, it was the parents, and not the daughters, that were put to the test!

Vocabulary List

Acampar – camping;

Adultos – adults, grown-ups;

Arrumaram – tidy up, arrange;

Brincadeiras – games that children play, from the verb "brincar" – "to play";

Cabeças – heads;

Cama – beds;

Desapontados – disappointed, bummed;

Despedida – a goodbye, from the verb "despedir" – "saying goodbye", but it can also refer to someone being fired, from the verb "despedir" – "to fire";

domingo – Sunday;

Estupendo – stupendous, stunning;

Euforia – euphoria, excitement;

Faculdade – college, faculty;

Habituado – used to something, accustomed;

Instruções – instructions, guidelines;

Juízo – literally it means "judgment", but it is usually used as it was in the text, meaning "behave" – "tenham juízo";

Juntas – together;

Mochilas – backpacks;

Motivação – motivation, drive;

Pais – parents;

Panela – pot, pan;

Pequenas – small, but also used to refer to someone when they were young/a child;

Portem-se (bem) – from the verb "portar" – "to behave", and is always followed by an adjective, characterizing how someone was behaving;

Primas – cousins;

Pulos – jumps;

Recepção – for instance, a hotel reception;

sábado – Saturday;

Saboroso – tasty, "delicioso";

Sacos – bags;

sexta-feira – Friday;

Tenda – tent;

Tentativa – a try, from the verb "to try" – "tentar";

Tios – uncles.

Perguntas

1. Porque estavam as primas tão contentes?
2. Qual foi o motivo que levou os pais a proporem aquela ideia?
3. Em que é que tiveram dificuldades as primas na primeira noite?
4. O que sentiram os pais no sábado?
5. Que lição aprenderam os pais?

Escolha Múltipla

1. Que idade tinham as primas?
   a) Catorze anos;
   b) Doze anos;
   c) Treze anos;
   d) Dez anos.

2. Que parte do corpo doeu às primas na hora da despedida?
   a) O coração;
   b) A barriga;
   c) A cabeça;
   d) O peito.
3. Onde jantaram os pais no sábado à noite?
   a) Num Restaurante;
   b) Na casa dos pais da Sara;
   c) Na casa dos pais da Ana;
   d) Na casa dos pais da Sofia;
4. Quantas horas dormiram as primas de sábado para domingo?
   a) Dormiram a noite toda;
   b) Doze horas;
   c) Dormiram só duas horas por causa dos mosquitos;
   d) Não dormiram.
5. Quem estava ansioso quando chegou a hora de voltar a casa?
   a) Os pais;
   b) Sara;
   c) Ana;
   d) Sofia.

Questions

1. Why were the cousins so happy?
2. What made the parents suggest this idea?
3. What was difficult in the first night?
4. How did the parents feel Saturday?
5. What lesson did the parents learn?

Multiple Choice

1. How old were the cousins?
   a) Fourteen;
   b) Twelve;
   c) Thirteen;
   d) Ten.

2. What part of the body ached when they were saying goodbye?
   a) The heart;
   b) The belly;
   c) The head;
   d) The chest.
3. Where did the parents have dinner Saturday night?
   a) At a restaurant;
   b) At Sara's parents' house;
   c) At Ana's parents' house;
   d) At Sofia's parents' house.
4. How many hours did the cousins sleep from Saturday to Sunday?
   a) They slept the whole night;
   b) Twelve hours;
   c) They only slept two hours because of the mosquitoes;
   d) They didn't sleep.
5. Who was anxious when it was time to come back home?
   a) The parents;
   b) Sara;
   c) Ana;
   d) Sofia.

Respostas

1. Porque iam acampar sozinhas.
2. Queriam que elas se habituassem a estar sozinhas para quando fossem para a faculdade.
3. Montar a tenda, a cozinhar, e a dormir.
4. Começaram a sentir-se saudades das filhas.
5. Que elas se iam habituar rápido e eles iam sentir mais falta das filhas do que estavam à espera.

Escolha Múltipla

1. a)
2. b)

3. c)
4. d)
5. a)

Answers

1. Because they were going camping by themselves.
2. They wanted them to be ready and used to being by themselves once they went to college.
3. Setting up the tent, cooking, and sleeping.
4. They started missing their daughters.
5. That they would get used to it quickly and they would miss their daughters more than they expected.

Multiple Choice

1. a)
2. b)
3. c)
4. d)
5. a)

Chapter 2 – Concurso de Castelos de Areia

A Teresa estava muito **aborrecida**. Ela estava a passear sozinha no **passeio** da rua da sua casa. Olhava para cima, para o lado, para o **chão**—não tinha nada mais divertido para fazer. Foi então que passou a Mariana, uma das suas amigas, que também morava naquela rua. Estava a sair de sua casa com uma **toalha** de praia e um **chapéu** nas mãos, e via-se que estava com muita pressa.

Teresa was very upset. She was walking alone on the sidewalk of her street. She would look up, look to the side, to the ground—she didn't have anything more fun to do. It was then that Mariana, one of her friends, who also lived on that street, passed by. She was leaving her house with a beach towel and hat on her hands, and Mariana could see that she was in a hurry.

– Olá... – saudou a Teresa.

– Olá, Teresinha! – respondeu a Mariana. – E adeus. – disse logo a seguir.

– Aonde vais? – insistiu a Teresa.

– Vou à praia. Hoje há um concurso de castelos de areia!

– Também quero participar! Vou contigo, pode ser? – decidiu a Teresa.

– Se quiseres… – respondeu Mariana com **indiferença**.

– Hello… – greeted Teresa.

– Hello, Teresinha! – answered Mariana. – And goodbye. – said immediately afterward.

– Where are you going? – insisted Teresa.

– I'm going to the beach. There is a sandcastle contest today!

– I also want to participate! I'm going with you, okay? – decided Teresa.

– If you want… – replied Mariana with indifference.

Quando Teresa e Mariana chegaram à praia, todos os seus amigos – Cátia, Filipe, Luísa, e Alberto –, já estavam lá.

When Teresa and Mariana arrived at the beach, all of their friends— Cátia, Filipe, Luísa, and Alberto—, were already there.

– Estás atrasada! – disse o Alberto à Mariana.

– Não faz mal! A **festa** só começa quando eu chegar. E o concurso também, naturalmente. – disse Mariana, **soltando** uma grande **gargalhada**.

– Também vais participar? – perguntou o Alberto à Teresa.

– A Teresa é muito pequena para fazer castelos de areia, eu acho que devia ficar a ver! – protestou a Mariana.

– Ninguém é muito pequeno para fazer castelos de areia. – disse o Alberto. – E se a Teresa não os começar a fazer agora, nunca mais aprenderá!

– You're late! – said Alberto to Mariana.

– It's okay! The party only starts when I get there. And the contest, too, of course. – said Mariana, with a huge laugh.

– Will you also participate? – Alberto asked Teresa.

– Teresa is too small to make sandcastles; I think she should just watch! – protested Mariana.

– Nobody is too small to make sandcastles. – Alberto said. – And if Teresa doesn't start making them now, she will never learn!

A Teresa era de todo o grupo de amigos a mais nova. O grupo era **composto** por quatro raparigas e dois rapazes. Filipe, Alberto, e Mariana tinham os três oito anos; Cátia e Luísa tinham 6 anos; Teresa tinha 4 anos. Por ser a mais nova, Teresa era sempre a menina que fazia todos os **favores** aos mais velhos, principalmente a Mariana, que estava sempre a pedir a Teresa que fizesse tudo o que Mariana tinha **preguiça** de fazer.

Teresa was the youngest in her group of friends. The group consisted of four girls and two boys. Filipe, Alberto, and Mariana were all 8 years old; Cátia and Luísa were 6 years old; Teresa was 4. Being the youngest, Teresa was always the girl who did all of the boring chores and tasks, especially Mariana's, who was always asking Teresa to do all of the things that Mariana was too lazy to do.

O grupo de amigos começou então a fazer castelos. A Teresa ficou **especada** a olhar para eles. Ela nunca tinha feito um castelo de areia, então não sabia bem por onde começar. Ficou uns segundos a olhar para eles para saber o que fazer primeiro. Como viu que todos estavam a fazer os seus castelos de areia à **beira-mar**, e não queria estar muito perto de Mariana para ela não **gozar** com o seu castelo, foi para um pouco mais longe. Mas assim que começou a construir o castelo, ele **desmanchou-se** todo!

The group of friends then began building the castles. Teresa was staring at them. She had never made a sandcastle, so she didn't know exactly where to start. She spent a few seconds staring at them to find out what to do first. Since everyone was making their sandcastles by the sea, and she did not want to be too close to Mariana, because she would start mocking her castle, Teresa moved a little farther away. But as soon as she started building the castle, it all collapsed!

– Como vais fazer um castelo de areia com areia seca? – disse a Mariana, aborrecida. – Eu até te ajudava, sendo que sou das melhores a fazer castelos de areia, mas estou muito **ocupada** a fazer o castelo vencedor!

– How are you going to make a sandcastle with dry sand? – said Mariana, bored. – I would help you, since I'm one of the best making sandcastles, but I'm too busy building the winning castle!

A Teresa ficou um bocadinho triste com esta **reprimenda** tão **brusca**. Foi então para beira-mar, para não repetir o erro que tinha cometido anteriormente. Começou por construir as muralhas do seu castelo. Estava **perto** de completar quatro muralhas, que se **ligavam** num quadrado, quando uma onda **embateu** contra o seu castelo. Tinha-se colocado tão perto da beira-mar que a água deitaria abaixo qualquer construção sua.

Teresa was a little upset due to this harsh reprimand. She then moved closer to the water, so she wouldn't repeat the mistake she had previously made. Teresa started building the walls of her castle. She was close to completing the four walls, which connected in a square, when a wave struck against her castle. Teresa was so near the water that it would destroy anything she built.

– Oh NÃO!!! **Fogo**, não vou conseguir construir um castelo... – exclamou Teresa, muito **desmotivada**.

– Oh NO!!! Dang, I will not be able to build a castle... – said Teresa, very demotivated.

Teresa ficou tão triste com este novo **azar** que quase começou a chorar. No entanto, recuperou as forças e decidiu que não ia desistir tão facilmente. Lembrou-se de Mariana e o quanto ela ia gozar com Teresa se a visse a chorar, então decidiu:

Teresa was so sad about this new misfortune that she almost started crying. Nevertheless, she regained her strength and decided that she would not give up so easily. She remembered Mariana and how she would make fun of Teresa if she saw her crying, so she decided:

– Vou tentar de novo!

– I'm going to try again!

Com **ânimo redobrado**, e mais motivada que nunca, Teresa encheu o balde com areia. Desta vez foi para um pouco mais longe da beira-mar, mas não tão longe que a areia não fosse molhada o suficiente para o castelo se aguentar em pé. Em primeiro lugar, fez as muralhas; depois, pôs uma torre em cada uma das esquinas. Acrescentou um castelo no meio, no qual construiu uma quinta torre no centro. Quando acabou, sentiu-se mesmo orgulhosa—tinha sido um caminho árduo para conseguir construir aquele castelo, mas ela tinha conseguido por nunca ter desistido e ter aprendido com os erros.

Full of vigor, and more motivated than ever, Teresa filled the bucket with sand. This time, she went to a spot farther away from the water, but not so far that the sand wasn't wet enough for the castle to stand upright. First of all, she built the walls; after that, she put a tower in each corner. She added a castle in the middle, in which she built a fifth tower right in the center. When it was done, she felt really proud—the road to build the castle was rough, but she had succeeded because she never gave up and because she had learned from her previous mistakes.

Para acabar em grande estilo, decidiu ainda por uma bandeira no topo do castelo. Ia espetá-la na torre que estava no centro do castelo. Para fazer a bandeira, procurou um pequeno pau com o tamanho ideal—nem muito grande nem muito pequeno. Encontrou um pau de gelado no meio da areia e com a tampa do iogurte que tinha comido ao **lanche**, fez assim a sua improvisada bandeira. Depois espetou-a no cimo da torre do centro do castelo, como tinha imaginado. Mas, sem querer, pôs uma mão no resto do castelo... e este **desmoronou-se** todo.

To end in style, she also decided to put a flag on top of the castle. Teresa was going to put it in the tower that was in the center of the castle. To make the flag, she looked for a small stick with the ideal size—neither too big nor too small. She found an ice cream stick that was in the middle of the sand, and with the lid of the yogurt she had eaten as a snack, she made this improvised flag. After that, she stuck it in the top of the tower that was in the center of the castle, just as she had imagined. But, unintentionally, Teresa put a hand on the rest of the castle... and it all went down.

– Tens que pôr mais areia na parte de baixo; senão, o castelo não fica bem apoiado! – exclamou a Mariana. – Eu até te ajudava...

– Olha, Teresa, não lhe dês ouvidos. – interveio o Alberto. – Se não é para ajudares, mais vale não dizeres nada, Mariana.

– A tentar é que se aprende. Não deves desanimar! Anda; eu ajudo-te a fazer uma base mais sólida. – disse Filipe.

– You have to put more sand at the bottom; otherwise, the castle is not stable! – said Mariana. – I would help you...

- Look, Teresa, don't listen to her. – intervened Alberto. – If you are not going to help, you might as well not say anything at all, Mariana.

– You only learn by trying. You must not get discouraged! Come on; I'll help you make a more stable foundation. – said Filipe.

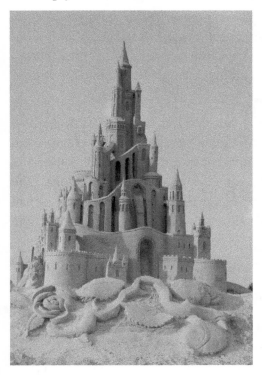

Cátia e Luísa estavam as duas a fazer o seu castelo de areia juntas. Como duas pessoas, eles construíram um castelo maior que os outros. A base era muito larga, cheia de areia. Filipe disse então a Teresa que era assim que ela deveria fazer também. Teresa, como não **desanimava** facilmente, voltou a tentar. Encheu de novo o seu balde com areia e começou a construir um novo castelo, com as dicas que tinha aprendido dos erros anteriores e dos seus amigos.

Cátia and Luisa were both making their sandcastle together. As two people, they made a castle way bigger than the others. The base was very wide, full of sand. Filipe then said to Teresa that this is how she should do it too. Teresa, as she didn't give up easily, tried again. She filled her bucket with sand and began to build a new castle, with the tips she had learned from her previous mistakes and from her friends.

Uns momentos depois, acabou, por fim, o seu castelo. Na verdade, era um castelo muito **estranho**! Tinha uma base gigante, e estava todo torto. Assim que deu uns passos para trás para ver o seu castelo, a Teresa achou que tinha que fazer algo para o tornar mais bonito. Recolheu todas as pequeninas coisas que conseguiu encontrar por ali perto e começou a enfeitar as muralhas com pedras, búzios, beatas, e conchas.

A few moments later, she finally finished her castle. In fact, it was a very weird-looking castle! It had a giant base, and it was all crooked. As soon as she took a few steps backward to look at her castle, Teresa thought she had to do something to make it prettier. She collected all the little things she could find around there and began adorning the castle walls with stones, whelks, cigarette butts, and shells.

– Já está! – disse com orgulho Teresa.

– It's done! – said Teresa, proudly.

Quando os amigos olharam para o castelo, não conseguiram esconder a expressão de surpresa.

When her friends looked at the castle, they couldn't hide an expression of surprise.

– É o castelo de areia feio que já vi até hoje! – exclamou logo Mariana, a rir.

– Até pode não ser o mais bonito – admitiu o Filipe –, mas de certeza que é o castelo mais resistente de todos. A base é mesmo larga. Além disso, gosto muito da decoração com as conchas.

– Pois, pois... Mas será que o castelo da Teresa pode participar no concurso sendo tão esquisito? – perguntou a Mariana.

– Claro que pode. Porque não havia de poder? – respondeu prontamente o Alberto.

– It is the ugliest castle that I have seen to this day! – said Mariana immediately, laughing.

– It might not to be the most beautiful – admitted Filipe –, but it sure is the most resilient castle of them all. The base is really wide. Besides, I really like the decoration with the shells.

– Right, right... But can Teresa's castle participate in the contest while being so weird? – asked Mariana.

– Of course it can. Why wouldn't it be able to? – answered Alberto swiftly.

Entretanto, os outros amigos também já tinham acabado os seus castelos. A Cátia e a Luísa tinham feito um castelo muito lindo. Tinham usado autocolantes dos seus livros, e no cimo de torre mais alta, tinham posto uma pena. O Alberto tinha feito um castelo com as muralhas redondas, o que era muito original. O Filipe tinha perdido algum tempo a ajudar a Teresa, por isso, o seu castelo estava muito básico—não tinha tido tempo para mais. Por fim, a Mariana tinha rodeado o seu castelo com um riacho cheio de água e tinha posto uma ponte levadiça feita com um pedaço de madeira na frente do castelo. Parecia uma miniatura de um verdadeiro castelo. Estavam todos os muitos entusiasmados a admirar os castelos uns dos outros, quando veio uma forte onda e os derrubou a todos. A todos, menos o a da Teresa.

Meanwhile, the other friends had also finished their castles. Cátia and Luisa had made a very beautiful castle. They had used stickers from their books, and at the top of the highest tower, they put a feather. Alberto had made a castle with round walls, which was very original. Filipe had wasted some time helping Teresa, so his castle was very basic—he didn't have time for more. Finally, Mariana had surrounded her castle with a stream full of water and put a drawbridge made with a piece of wood on the front of the castle. It looked like a miniature of a real castle. All were enthusiastic and admiring each other's castles when a strong wave came and destroyed all of the castles. All, but Teresa's.

– O castelo da Teresa podia até não ser o mais bonito – comentou o Filipe –, mas é sem dúvida o mais resistente de todos!

– Tens razão! A vencedora do concurso é... a Teresa! – gritou o Alberto.

– Mas o meu era o melhor de todos! Eu é que sou a vencedora! – reclamou a Mariana.

– Bem, na verdade, Mariana, o castelo da Teresa é o ÚNICO castelo a concorrer... – disse a Cátia.

– Além disso, a Teresa merece o prémio, porque demonstrou muita imaginação, e ainda mais importante, nunca desistiu! – acrescentou a Luísa.

– Teresa's castle might not have been the most beautiful – said Filipe –, but it is by far the toughest of them all!

– You're right! The winner of the contest is... Teresa! – shouted Alberto.

– But mine was the best of them all! I am the winner! – complained Mariana.

– Well, in fact, Mariana, Teresa's castle is the ONLY castle that is competing... – said Cátia.

– Besides, Teresa deserves the prize because she showed a lot of imagination, and more importantly, she never gave up! – added Luísa.

Sumário

Teresa e Mariana participaram num concurso de castelos de areia na praia. Mariana era muito boa, conseguindo construir belos castelos. Teresa era um pouco inexperiente, e os seus castelos não eram muito bonitos. Por não ter muita experiência a construir castelos, teve que passar por um duro processo de aprendizagem para conseguir fazer um castelo que fosse apropriado. Apesar de não ser o mais bonito, o castelo que a Teresa construi tinha outras qualidades que o castelo de Mariana não possuía. Assim, na hora de entregar o prémio ao castelo vencedor, a Mariana apanhou uma grande surpresa...

Summary

Teresa and Mariana were participating in a contest of sandcastles on the beach. Mariana was very good at it, and was able to build beautiful castles. Teresa was a bit inexperienced, and her castles were not very pretty. Because she didn't have much experience building castles, she had to go through a hard learning process to get a castle that was appropriate. Although not the most beautiful, the castle that Teresa built had other qualities that the castle of Mariana did not possess. So, when the time of handing the prize to the winning castle came, Mariana was up for a big surprise...

Vocabulary List

Aborrecida – bored, annoyed, upset;

Ânimo – spirit, mood;

Azar – bad luck, misfortune;

Beira-mar – in the beach or a sidewalk, right by the sea, waterfront;

Balde – bucket;

Brusca – abrupt, sudden, harsh, blunt;

Chão – floor, ground;

Chapéu – hat, cap;

Composto – composed, comprised, formed;

Desanimar – discourage, lose heart, dispirited;

Desmanchou-se – dissolved, fell down, came apart;

Desmoronou-se – collapsed, dissolved, came apart, landslide;

Desmotivada – discouraged, dispirited;

Embateu – clashed, struck;

Especada – still, motionless;

Estranho – weird, strange, odd;

Festa – party, festival;

Fogo – it can be used as an interjection, but literally it means "fire";

Gargalhada – a really loud and genuine laugh;

Gozar – to mock, to tease, but also to enjoy;

Indiferença – indifference, nonchalance;

Lanche – snack, small meal, usually in the middle of the afternoon;

Ligavam – connected, but it can also mean "called", as you'd call somebody on the phone;

Ocupada – busy, occupied;

Passeio – sidewalk, but it can also be used as "taking a walk" – "dar um passeio";

Perto – close, near;

Preguiça – laziness, but also used for the animal "sloth";

Redobrado – doubled, reinforced, intensified;

Reprimenda – reprimand, scolding;

Soltando – to let go of something;

Toalha – towel.

Perguntas

1. Porque ia Mariana para a praia?
2. A Mariana opunha-se a que Teresa participasse no concurso. Porquê?
3. Qual foi o primeiro erro de Teresa ao construir um castelo?
4. Escreva três traços de personalidade que caracterizam a Teresa.
5. Porque ganhou Teresa o concurso?

Escolha Múltipla

1. Quem era a pessoa mais nova do grupo de amigos?
   a) Alberto;
   b) Filipe;
   c) Cátia;
   d) Teresa.
2. Porque foi Teresa fazer o seu primeiro castelo para longe dos amigos?
   a) Porque gostava de estar sozinha;
   b) Porque achou aquele sítio melhor;
   c) Porque não queria que Mariana gozasse com o seu castelo;
   d) Porque não havia espaço.
3. Quantas torres tinha o penúltimo castelo de Teresa?
   a) Nenhuma;
   b) Cinco;
   c) Quatro;
   d) Três;
4. Qual dos amigos saiu prejudicado por ajudar Teresa?
   a) Filipe;
   b) Cátia;
   c) Mariana;
   d) Alberto.
5. O que usou Teresa para decorar o seu castelo?

a) Brinquedos;
b) Algas;
c) Autocolantes;
d) Conchas e búzios.

Questions

1. Why was Mariana going to the beach?
2. Mariana was opposed to Teresa participating in the contest. Why?
3. What was Teresa's first mistake when building the first castle?
4. Write down three personality traits that characterize Teresa.
5. Why did Teresa win the contest?

Multiple Choice

1. Who was the youngest of the group of friends?
   a) Alberto;
   b) Filipe;
   c) Cátia;
   d) Teresa.

2. Why did Teresa go far away from her friends to make the first castle?
   a) Because she liked being alone;
   b) Because she thought that spot was better;
   c) Because she didn't want Mariana to mock her;
   d) Because there was no space.
3. How many towers did Teresa's second-to-last castle have?
   a) None;
   b) Five;
   c) Four;
   d) Three.
4. Which friend was at a disadvantage for helping Teresa?
   a) Filipe;
   b) Cátia;

c) Mariana;

d) Alberto.

5. What did Teresa use to decorate her castle?

  a) Toys;

  b) Seaweed;

  c) Stickers;

  d) Whelks and shells.

Respostas

1. Porque havia um concurso de castelos de areia na praia.
2. Porque achava que ela era muito nova.
3. Usou areia muito seca.
4. Persistente, lutadora, trabalhadora (mas outras respostas também são possíveis).
5. Porque era o único que tinha sobrevivido à onda que derrubou todos os outros castelos.

Escolha Múltipla

1. d)
2. c)
3. b)
4. a)
5. d)

Answers

1. Because there was a sandcastle contest at the beach.
2. Because she thought Teresa was too young.
3. She used dry sand.
4. Persistent, fighter, hard-working (but other answers are also possible).
5. Because it was the only one standing after the wave destroyed every other castle.

Multiple Choice

1. d)

2. c)
3. b)
4. a)
5. d)

Chapter 3 – O Viajante Américo

Américo era uma formiga jovem e de todas a mais **trabalhadora**. Durante o Verão tinha trabalhado muito, tal como a sua família, para poderem ter comida no Inverno. Por isso, andava cansado e precisava de **repousar**.

Américo was a young ant, and out of them all, the one that worked the hardest. During summer, he had worked hard, just like his family, so they could have food during the winter. So, he was tired and needed to rest.

– Tens que ir **férias**, Américo – a mãe dele disse. – Precisas de descansar!

– Eu estou de **acordo**! – disse o pai.

– Vai, Américo, diverte-te! E não te esqueças de me trazeres **prendas**! – disse o seu irmão Fumiga.

– You have to go on a vacation, Américo – his mother said. – You need to rest!

– I agree! – said the dad.

– Go, Américo, have fun! And don't forget to bring me gifts! – said his brother Fumiga.

Ele não podia ir com ele porque era muito pequenino ainda. Além disso, havia festas na terra e concursos a que Fumiga nunca tinha faltado – e esta não iria ser a primeira vez. Américo foi fazer a sua **mala** de viagem. Como gostava bastante de pintar, pegou na **caixa** das tintas e no lanche que a mãe lhe preparara e partiu.

Ao chegar a um bosque com árvores muito altas, respirou fundo:

He couldn't go with him because he was still too small. Besides, there were parties and contests on their village that Fumiga had never missed—and this wouldn't be the first time. Américo went to pack his bag for the trip. Since he liked painting a lot, he took the box of paints and the snacks that his mother prepared for him and left.

When he got to a wood with very tall trees, he took a deep breath:

– Que boa vida! Que bem se respira! Aqui todos são felizes, tenho a certeza!

– What a good life! So easy to breathe! Here everyone is happy, I am sure!

Então pareceu-lhe ouvir chorar. Olhou à volta dele, e foi então que finalmente viu que em cima de um cogumelo, estava uma borboleta a chorar, dizendo:

Then he thought he heard someone crying. He looked around, and then finally he saw that on top of a mushroom, there was a butterfly crying and saying:

– Oh, não! Vê só o que me fez um menino com a sua **rede** de apanhar borboletas!

– Não te preocupes bonita borboleta; eu vou ajudar-te! – disse o Américo.

– Oh, muito obrigada, cara formiga! O que posso fazer por ti? – disse a borboleta.

– Tu és muito bonita e tens muitas cores nas tuas asas. Posso pintar o teu **retrato**? – perguntou Américo.

– Claro! – disse logo a borboleta.

– Oh, no! Just look at what a boy has done to me with his net for catching butterflies!

– Don't worry, beautiful butterfly; I will help you! – said Américo.

– Oh, thank you, dear ant! What can I do for you? – said the butterfly.

– You are very pretty and have many colors in your wings. Can I paint your portrait? – asked Américo.

– Of course! – said promptly the butterfly.

Américo começou então a pintar no seu caderno a sua nova amiga. As suas asas tinham verde, azul, amarelo, e roxo nelas. Era incrível. Parecia quase um **arco-íris**! Quando finalmente acabou, a borboleta agradeceu mais uma vez a ajuda e foi embora.

Américo then started to paint his new friend on his notebook. Her wings had green, blue, yellow, and purple in them. It was incredible. It almost seemed like a rainbow! When he was finally done, the butterfly thanked him once more and left.

Pouco a pouco, ia **escurecendo**. Américo estava sentado debaixo de uma árvore e tentava dormir, mas não conseguia. Tinha medo do

escuro e das sombras que fazia a **Lua**. Ao longe, via qualquer coisa a **piscar** – aproximava-se um **pirilampo**, com a sua luz acesa, que se ofereceu para lhe fazer companhia durante a noite. Só assim o Américo conseguiu adormecer.

Little by little, it was getting dark. Américo was sitting under a tree and trying to fall asleep, but he couldn't. He was afraid of the dark and of the shadows made by the moon. He saw something flashing— a firefly was approaching, with his light on, and offered to keep him company overnight. It was only then that Américo was able to sleep.

Quando acordou, o sol brilhava e estava muito calor. Mas logo, lhe caiu uma **gota** de água na cara, e outra e outra ainda. "Está a chover", pensou, surpreendido. Olhou para o céu, e o sol continuava a brilhar. Então descobriu a origem das gotas de água: pousado num ramo, um passarinho chorava. Era um pintarroxo. Mas um pintarroxo que não tinha **peito** avermelhado como os outros da sua espécie—o seu peito era branco, e por isso, chorava.

When he woke up, the sun was shining, and it was really hot. But soon, a drop of water fell on his face, and another and yet another. "It's raining," he thought, surprised. He looked up at the sky, and the sun kept shining. Then he discovered the origin of the water droplets: on a branch, a little bird was crying. It was a linnet. But a linnet who had no reddish chest, unlike the other birds of his species—his chest was white, and for that, it was crying.

– Não te preocupes, meu amigo – disse Américo – eu trato disso!

– Don't worry, my friend – said Américo – I'll take care of that!

Então Américo pegou num **pincel** e na tinta vermelha e pintou o peito do passarinho. O passarinho ficou tão contente que não conseguia parar de cantar. Perguntou ao Américo o que podia fazer por ele, e Américo pediu-lhe se podia pintar o retrato dele, e assim fez. Pegou então no seu caderno de **desenho** e desenhou o belo passarinho. Desenhou as **penas**, o **bico**, as pequenas **patas**, a cabeça, e o peito vermelho. Pouco tempo depois de ter acabado, chegou a fêmea do pintarroxo que andava à procura dele, e partiram os dois.

So Américo took out his brush and the red paint and painted the bird's chest. The little bird was so happy that he couldn't stop singing. He asked Américo what he could do for him, and Américo asked if he could paint his portrait, and so he did. He took out his sketchbook and painted the beautiful little bird. He painted the feathers, the beak, the small paws, the head, and the red chest. Not long after the portrait was finished, the female linnet who was looking for him came, and the two left.

Américo continuou também as suas férias. Estava a andar pela floresta, em busca de um lago para pintar e beber água quando caiu num **buraco**. Magoou a cabeça nas pedras e, quando olhou para cima, viu o céu lá no alto. Pensou que já não conseguiria sair daquele buraco, quando ouviu uma vozinha que dizia:

Américo went on with his holidays as well. He was walking along the forest, in search of a lake to paint and drink a bit of water when he fell down a hole. He hurt his head on the rocks, and when he looked up, he saw the sky high above. He thought he wouldn't be able to get out of that hole when he heard a little voice saying:

– Não te preocupes amigo. Vou tirar-te daí.

– Don't worry, buddy. I'm going to get you out of there.

De um pequeno túnel saiu uma toupeira. Fora ela que falara. Aquele túnel era o caminho que levava à sua casa. Américo saiu do buraco através do túnel. Por fim, chegaram a casa da Toupeira. A casa era muito grande e bonita e tinha uma família **encantadora**: além do Sr. Toupeira, estava lá a Sra. Toupeira, e os filhos Topix, Topal, e o Toupinha Jr. Equanto, a sra. Toupeira preparava a Américo uma chávena de chá de ervas aromáticas com mel que o ia ajudar com a dor de cabeça, e os filhos divertiam-se, **sacudindo** as calças de Américo para lhes tirar a **terra**. Depois, comeram uma **bela** refeição. Américo claro, pediu-lhes ainda se podia pintar a sua bela casa.

Out of a small tunnel came a mole. It was this mole that had spoken. That tunnel was the path to his house. Finally, they arrived at the mole's house. His home was very large and beautiful, and he had a lovely family: besides Mr. Mole, there was Mrs. Mole and the children Topix, Topal, and Toupinha Jr. Meanwhile, Mrs. Mole prepared Américo a cup of aromatic herbal tea with honey to help with his headache, and the children were having fun, shaking Américo's pants to get the dirt off of them. Afterward, they ate a fine meal. Américo, of course, asked if he could paint their beautiful home.

Quando acabou a pintura, Américo despediu-se dos seus bons amigos, agradeceu e foi-se embora. Correu e passeou pelo bosque até ficar cansado. Foi então que sentiu fome e percebeu que tinha perdido a comida no buraco.

When he finished his painting, Américo said goodbye to his good friends, he thanked them and left. He ran and walked along the woods until he was tired. It was then that he felt hungry and realized he had left his snacks in the hole.

– Tenho tanta fome! – disse em voz alta.

– I'm so hungry! – said Américo out loud.

Um esquilo que estava por perto à procura de nozes, pinhões e outros frutos do bosque, ouvi-o. Tinha de guardar comida para o Inverno, mas não queria deixar aquela pobre formiga com fome. Disse então a Américo que podiam ir a casa dele para comer qualquer coisa. Américo agradeceu, mas sabendo que o esquilo deveria precisar de comida para o Inverno, dispôs-se logo a ajudá-lo a recolher comida. Quando finalmente foram para casa depois de trabalhar, o esquilo ofereceu-lhe um grande ovo e um copo de leite! Américo agradeceu mais uma vez e foi-se embora.

A squirrel that was nearby looking for walnuts, pine nuts, and other wood nuts, heard him. He had to save food for the winter, but he didn't want to leave that poor ant that hungry. She then told Américo that they could go to his house to eat something. Américo said thank you, but he knew the squirrel probably needed food for the winter, so he immediately offered his help to collect food. When they finally headed home after working, the squirrel offered him a big tree leaf and a glass of water! Américo thanked him once more and left.

Já a caminhar pelo bosque, Américo apercebeu-se que não tinha parado um só instante desde o início das férias. Pensou que era melhor voltar para casa. Neste bosque, não iria conseguir descansar.

Already walking through the woods, Américo realized he hadn't rested for a second since the beginning of the holidays. He thought it was better to return home. In these woods, he wouldn't be able to rest.

Quando Américo chegou a casa, a sua família ficou muito contente. Todos tinham muitas coisas para lhe contar, mas primeiro, perguntaram como tinha sido a viagem. Américo mostrou à família os desenhos que tinha feito e todos ficaram encantados. A **notícia** correu pelo bosque, e todos os animais quiseram ver os famosos desenhos de Américo. Até os novos amigos que tinha feito se quiseram juntar a eles: a borboleta, os pintarroxos, o pirilampo, a família Toupeira, e o esquilo. Depois de uma grande refeição, todos se foram embora, e o Américo deitou-se na cama que o pai lhe tinha preparado no jardim e adormeceu! Por fim, tinha conseguido umas férias... no jardim de sua casa.

When Américo got home, his family was really happy. All of them had many things to tell him, but first, they asked how his trip had been. Américo showed his family the paintings he had done, and everyone was amazed. The news went around the woods, and every animal wanted to see Américo's famous paintings. Even his new friends wanted to join him: the butterfly, the linnets, the firefly, the Mole family, and the squirrel. After a big meal, everyone left, and Américo lay on the bed his dad had made for him on the garden and fell asleep! At last, he got his holidays... in his house's garden.

Sumário

Américo era uma formiga muito trabalhadora. Tinha trabalhado todo o Verão para poder ter comida suficiente no Inverno. Ficou tão cansado que a sua família lhe disse que era melhor ele ir de férias para descansar. Então, lá foi Américo para o bosque para relaxar. Como gostava muito de pintar, levou os seus pincéis e tintas, e ao longo das aventuras das suas férias, teve a oportunidade de pintar vários retratos. Toda essa prática fez com que ele melhorasse muito as suas capacidades – algo que todos os animais do bosque confirmaram!

Summary

Américo was a very hard-working ant. He had worked all summer so he could have enough food in the winter. He got so tired that his family told him he'd better go on vacation to rest. So, there went Américo to the woods, to relax. Since he liked to paint, he took his paintbrushes and paints, and throughout the adventures of his holiday, he had the opportunity to paint several portraits. All of that practice made him greatly improve his abilities—something every animal from the woods confirmed!

Vocabulary List

(de) Acordo – agreed, it's a deal;

Arco-íris – rainbow;

Bela – beautiful, gorgeous, lovely;

Bico – beak, nozzle;

Buraco – hole, gap;

Caixa – box, case;

Desenhos – drawings, paintings;

Encantadora –charming, delightful;

Escurecendo – getting dark, the sun fading away;

Escuro – dark, dim;

Férias – vacation, holidays;

Gota – drop, droplet;

Lua – moon

Mala – suitcase, bag, backpack;

Notícia – news;

Patas – paws, hoofs, legs;

Peito – chest, breasts;

Penas – feathers, but it can also mean "pity", as in you'd feel "pity for someone" – "pena de alguém";

Pincel – brush;

Pirilampo – firefly;

Piscar – blinking, winking, flashing;

Prendas – gift, presents, treats;

Rede – net, network;

Repousar – rest, relax, lie down;

Retrato – portrait;

Sacudindo – shaking, rattling, rocking;

Terra – earth, land, small village;

Trabalhadora – very hard worker;

Viajante – Traveler, voyager.

Perguntas

1. Porque precisava Américo de ir de férias?
2. De que animal do bosque Américo pintou o retrato primeiro?
3. Porque estava a chorar o passarinho?
4. Porque voltou Américo a casa?
5. O que fez os animais todos irem a casa de Américo?

Escolha Múltipla

1. Fumiga, o irmão de Américo, não foi com ele. Porquê?
   a) Era muito novo;
   b) Não queria ir;
   c) Tinha de trabalhar;
   d) Tinha de ir à escola.
2. Onde estava poisada a borboleta?
   a) Numa flor;
   b) Num galho;
   c) Num cogumelo;
   d) Numa pedra.
3. Quais eram as cores das asas da borboleta?
   a) Roxo, preto, verde, branco;
   b) Verde, azul, amarelo, roxo;
   c) Verde, amarelo, vermelho, azul;
   d) Amarelo, azul, castanho;
4. O que deu a Sra. Toupeira a Américo para ajudar com a dor de cabeça?
   a) Um café;
   b) Leite com canela;
   c) Um copo de vinho;
   d) Um chá com mel.
5. O que comeu Américo na casa das Toupeiras?
   a) Um grande ovo;
   b) Um copo de leite;
   c) Cajús;

d) Amêndoas.

Questions

1. Why did Américo need to go on a vacation?
2. What forest animal did Américo paint the portrait of first?
3. Why was the little bird crying?
4. Why did Américo return home?
5. Why did all the animals go to Américo's house?

Multiple Choice

1. Fumiga, Américo's brother, couldn't go with him. Why?
    a) He was too young;
    b) He didn't want to;
    c) He had to work;
    d) He had to go to school.

2. What was the butterfly standing on?
    a) Flower;
    b) Twig;
    c) Mushroom;
    d) Rock.

3. What were the colors on the butterfly's wings?
    a) Purple, black, green, white;
    b) Green, blue, yellow, purple;
    c) Green, yellow, red, blue;
    d) Yellow, blue, brown.

4. What did Mrs. Mole give Américo to help with the headache?
    a) A coffee;
    b) Milk with cinnamon;
    c) A glass of wine;
    d) A tea with honey.

5. What did Américo eat at the Mole family's house?
    a) A big egg;
    b) A glass of milk;

c) Cashews;
d) Almonds.

Respostas

1. Porque tinha trabalhado muito e precisava de descansar.
2. A borboleta.
3. Porque era um pintarroxo, mas não tinha o peito vermelho como os outros pintarroxos.
4. Porque não conseguia descansar no bosque.
5. Porque queriam ver os famosos desenhos de Américo.

Escolha Múltipla

1.)
2. c)
3. b)
4. d)
5. a)

Answers

1. Because he had worked a lot and needed to rest.
2. The butterfly.
3. Because he was a linnet, but he didn't have a reddish chest like the other linnets.
4. Because he wasn't able to rest properly in the woods.
5. Because they wanted to see Américo's famous drawings.

Multiple Choice

1. a)
2. c)
3. b)
4. d)
5. a)

Chapter 4 – O Pão Mais Saboroso

– Só temos fiambre para pôr no pão! – disse Carla, a mãe de Zé.

– O que é isto? Não quero comer isto! Pior só comer o pão sem nada por dentro! – **resmungou** Zé.

– Ai este rapaz, tão **esquisito**. Mas a culpa é toda minha! O que é que queres comer então? – perguntou a mãe.

– Quero uma sandes de ovo **cozido**, com maionese **caseira**, alface e tomate, e milho. – respondeu Zé, a salivar.

– Mas não tenho isso tudo aqui agora! E maionese caseira? Não comes se não for caseira? – disse a mãe, quase em **desespero**.

– Não, Mãe, a tua sabe muito melhor! – disse Zé, a tentar **convencer** a mãe.

– We only have ham to put in the bread! – said Carla, Zé's mother.

– What is this? I don't want to eat this! There is only one thing that is worse than this, and that is eating the bread with nothing in it! – protested Zé.

– Oh, this boy, so picky. But the fault is all mine. What do you want to eat, then? – asked the mother.

– I want an egg sandwich, with homemade mayonnaise, lettuce, tomato, and corn. – answered Zé, salivating.

– But I don't have all of that at home now! And homemade mayonnaise? You won't eat it unless it is homemade? – said the mother, almost in despair.

– No, Mom, yours tastes better! – said Zé, trying to persuade his mom.

Depois de uns minutos nisto, a mãe acabou por **ceder**. Zé já sabia como era—bastava insistir um bocadinho, e a mãe acabava por ceder. Das raras vezes que dizia que não, Zé punha uma cara triste, recusava a comida que a mãe lhe dava em alternativa, depois dizia que tinha fome, e a mãe lá ia preparar o que o filho queria em primeiro lugar. Sempre tinha sido assim, e agora Carla sentia que já era tarde para mudar. Nem ela conseguia dizer que não ao filho, nem o filho fazia um **esforço** para se adaptar. Ao menos, podia ser ele a fazer a própria comida, mas não! Era sempre algo especial, e tinha que ser sempre a mãe.

After a few minutes of this, the mom ended up giving in. Zé knew how it worked—he just had to be insistent, and his mom would always end up giving in. The few times she said no, Zé would put on a sad face, refuse the food his mom gave him instead, then say he was hungry, and the mother would go and make what the son wanted in the first place. It had always been like that, and now Carla thought it was too late to change anything. She wasn't able to say no to her son, and the son didn't try to adapt. He could, at least, be the one that was preparing his own food, but no! It always had to be something special, and it always had to be his mother preparing it.

O pai de Zé, Ricardo, achava que isto tudo era um **exagero**. Ricardo, no entanto, era um homem **calado** que **raramente** dava a sua opinião. Quando estavam à mesa, o pai olhava para os dois com uma expressão de **reprovação**, mas nada dizia. Era um homem de acções e poucas palavras. Decidiu então dar uma lição valiosa a Zé— custava-lhe ver a mulher, que não ia para nova a ter tanto trabalho para cuidar de um rapaz crescido. Mas mais do que isso, não gostava nada de ver o seu filho, que se estava a tornar um homem, a ser tão **mimado** e a não saber cuidar de si.

Zé's dad, Ricardo, thought that this was all too much. Ricardo was, however, a very quiet man who always kept his opinion to himself. When they were at the table, the father would look to both with an expression of disapproval, but he wouldn't say anything. He was a man of action, not of words. He then decided to teach Zé a valuable lesson—it was hard for him to see his wife that wasn't getting any younger, having so much work while caring for a grown-up boy. But more than that, he really didn't like that his son, who was becoming a man, was so spoiled and that he didn't know how to take care of himself.

O pai **tossiu** então duas vezes, que era o sinal de que ia falar, e tanto a mãe como o filho se calaram. Disse então o pai:

The dad then coughed twice, which was the signal indicating he was going to speak, and both mother and son stopped talking. Then, the dad said:

– Amanhã vens trabalhar comigo para o **campo**. Passa lá à hora de almoço um homem que vende o melhor pão do mundo. Quando provares aquilo, não vais querer outra coisa para o resto da vida.

– A sério, Pai? Óptimo! Quero ir! Mas tenho mesmo que trabalhar? – **queixou-se** Zé.

– Ai este rapaz, não quer fazer nada, que preguiçoso! – disse a mãe.

– De qualquer maneira, se vais, não te faz mal nenhum ajudar aqui o teu velhote. – respondeu o pai.

– Tomorrow, you are going to come with me to work in the field. By lunchtime, a man that sells the best bread in the world passes by. When you taste that, you will not want anything else for the rest of your life.

– Really, Dad? Great! I want to go! But do I really have to work? – complained Zé.

– Oh, this boy, he doesn't want to do anything, so lazy! – said the mother.

– Since you're going anyway, it won't hurt giving your old man a hand. – answered the dad.

Então, no dia seguinte, pai e filho, de saco às costas, lá foram para o campo trabalhar. Trabalharam **arduamente** a manhã inteira, e o filho não se saiu nada mal. Tinha um corpo atlético e bom para trabalhar, o que era natural porque comia muito bem. Perto já da hora de almoço, pai e filho começaram a ficar **esfomeados.** O Zé já estava a salivar só de pensar no melhor pão do mundo que o pai lhe prometera.

So, the following day, father and son, each with a backpack, went to the field to work. They worked strenuously throughout the whole morning, and the son wasn't doing bad at all. He had an athletic body that was good to work, which was natural since he ate so well. When it was near lunchtime, father and son were starting to get really hungry. Zé was already salivating just by thinking about the best bread in the world that his dad promised him.

– Então pai, quando chega o senhor do pão? – perguntou o filho, já **ansioso**.

– Já deve estar aí a vir… – respondeu o pai, calmamente.

– So, dad, when does the man with the bread get here? – asked the son, already anxious.

– He must be here any minute now… – answered the dad, calmly.

Entretanto, continuaram a trabalhar. Mais umas horas se passaram, e o senhor do pão ainda não tinha chegado. Zé começava já a ficar **exasperado**, mas o seu pai mantinha uma calma **estóica**. O filho perguntava **incessantemente**:

Meanwhile, they kept working. A few more hours went by, and the man with the bread had still not yet arrived. Zé was beginning to despair, but his dad was super calm. The son asked, relentlessly:

– Pai, quando chega o senhor? Já passa da hora de almoço!

– Já deve estar aí a vir… – respondia o pai.

– Dad, when does the man get here? It's long past lunchtime!

– He must be here any minute now…. – would answer the dad.

Até que o dia começava já a escurecer, e nada do senhor do pão. O filho estava absolutamente esfomeado. Tinha tanta fome que nem conseguia **reclamar** com o pai por o senhor não ter aparecido. Foi então que o pai tirou do seu saco dois pães. Deu um ao filho e começou a comer o outro. Zé estava tão cansado que começou a comer o seu pão também, sem sequer perguntar, como sempre fazia, o que levava dentro.

The day started to become darker and darker, and the man with the bread was nowhere to be seen. The son was absolutely famished. He was so hungry that he wasn't even able to say anything to his dad about the man not showing up. It was then that the dad took out of his bag two pieces of bread. He gave one to his son and started eating the other. Zé was so tired that he started eating his bread as well, without even asking, as he always did, what was inside it.

Quando Zé acabou de comer, o pai perguntou:

When Zé finished eating, the dad asked:

– Sabes o que levava o pão?

– Não sei; só sei que foi o melhor pão que já comi na minha vida!

– Então ficas a saber: não levava nada, filho. O trabalho e a fome, fazem qualquer coisa saber bem, e nós temos o **privilégio** de ter muitas coisas à escolha para comer, mas nem toda a **gente** pode dizer o mesmo. Por isso, temos que saber dar valor ao que temos.

– Do you know what was in the bread?

– I don't know; I only know that it was the best bread I have ever eaten in my life!

– So, now you know: there wasn't anything in it, son. Work and hunger make anything taste delicious, and we have the privilege of having many things to choose to eat from, but not everybody can say the same thing. Because of that, we have to value what we have.

O filho aprendeu a lição, e desde então, aceitou sempre o que a mãe lhe dava para comer.

The son learned his lesson, and from that day on, he always accepted whatever his mom gave him to eat.

Sumário

Zé é um rapaz que come muito mas que é muito esquisito. A sua comida tem sempre de ser especial. O pai, pronto a ensinar-lhe uma lição, diz-lhe para ir com ele trabalhar um dia para o campo, que lá passa sempre um homem à hora de almoço com o pão mais saboroso do mundo. O filho, entusiasmado, acede, e no dia seguinte lá vão os dois para o campo trabalhar. O trabalho no campo é árduo, e ao aproximar-se a hora de almoço, os dois estão já esfomeados. Porém, o homem naquele dia estava atrasado. O pai e filho vão ficando com cada vez mais fome. À medida que o tempo vai passando e o dia escurecendo, a fome não lhes permite aguentar mais o trabalho. É então que o pai tira do saco dois pães e dá um ao filho. Este fica deliciado já que se apercebe que acaba de comer a melhor refeição da vida dele.

Summary

Zé is a boy that eats a lot but is very picky. His food always has to be special. His dad, eager to teach him a lesson, tells him to go and work with him in the field one day, since a man that has the best bread in the world passes by around lunchtime. The son, excited, agrees, and the next day, both go to the field to work. The work in the field is hard, and when lunchtime came, both were already starving. However, the man was late that day. Father and son are hungrier and hungrier. As time goes by, and the day ends, their hunger doesn't allow them to carry on working. It is then that the father gets two buns out of his bag, giving one to the son. The son is delighted since he realizes he just ate the best meal of his life.

Vocabulary List

Ansioso – anxious, eager, keen;

Arduamente – hard, strenuously;

Calado – it describes somebody who is not speaking, but when used as an adjective, it means "quiet";

Campo – field, countryside;

Caseira – homemade, homey;

Ceder – giving in, breaking, yield, compromise;

Convencer – to persuade, to convince, win over;

Cozido – boiled;

Desespero – despair, distress;

Esfomeado – starving, famished;

Esforço – effort, struggle;

Esquisito – picky, weird, strange, awkward;

Estóica – stoic;

Exagero – exaggeration, overdo, overindulge;

Exasperado – exasperated, despaired, panicked;

Gente – crowd, people;

Incenssantemente – non-stop, relentlessly;

Mimado – spoiled, pampered;

Privilégio – privilege;

Queixou-se – complained;

Raramente – rarely, scarcely;

Reclamar – to complain, to talk back to someone in a rude way;

Reprovação – disapproval, condemnation;

Resmungou – grumbled, muttered;

Tossiu – coughed.

Perguntas

1. Sobre o que falam mãe e filho no primeiro parágrafo?
2. Porque Zé era tão esquisito com a comida?
3. O que disse o pai sobre o assunto?
4. Por que motivo não passou o homem do pão?
5. Porque soube o pão sem nada tão bem a Zé?

Escolha Múltipla

1. O que queria Zé na sua sandes?
   a) Carne assada;
   b) Ovos mexidos e ketchup;
   c) Fiambre e queijo;
   d) Ovo cozido e maionese caseira.

2. Que sinal fazia Ricardo para mostrar que ia falar?
   a) Tossia;
   b) Coçava a barba;
   c) Arrotava;
   d) Falava mais alto.

3. O corpo do Zé era tal como o de um...?
   a) Um bailarino;
   b) Um trabalhador das obras;
   c) Um desportista;
   d) Um rei gordo;

4. Quando comeram o pão Zé e Ricardo?
   a) Ao almoço;
   b) Ao jantar;
   c) Quando o dia começou a escurecer;
   d) Quando voltaram a casa.

5. O que estava dentro do pão?
   a) Ovo cozido e maionese caseira;
   b) Um bife;
   c) Presunto;

d) Nada.

Questions

1. What are mother and son talking about in the first paragraph?

2. Why was Zé so picky with the food?

3. What did the father say about the matter?

4. Why didn't the man that sold the bread come?

5. Why did the bread taste so good to Zé?

Multiple Choice

1. What did Zé want in his sandwich?
   a) Roasted meat;
   b) Scrambled eggs and ketchup;
   c) Ham and cheese;
   d) Boiled egg and homemade mayonnaise.

2. What signal did Ricardo make to show that he was going to talk?
   a) Coughed;
   b) Scratched his beard;
   c) Burped;
   d) He spoke louder.

3. Was Zé's body just like a...?
   a) A dancer;
   b) A worker;
   c) A sportsman;
   d) A fat king.

4. When did Zé and Ricardo eat the bread?
   a) At lunch;
   b) At dinner;
   c) When the day began to darken;
   d) When they came home.

5. What was in the bread?
   a) Cooked egg and homemade mayonnaise;
   b) A steak;

c) Ham;
d) Nothing.

Respostas

1. Estão a falar sobre o que Zé quer na sandes dele.
2. Porque a mãe o tinha habituado mal.
3. No início nada. Depois, disse ao filho que iam trabalhar para o campo no dia seguinte.
4. Porque era mentira, não havia homem do pão.
5. Porque estava cheio de fome e cansado.

Escolha Múltipla

1. d)
2. a)
3. b)
4. c)
5. d)

Answers

1. They are talking about what Zé wants in his sandwich.
2. Because his mother had spoiled him.
3. At the beginning, nothing. Then, he said he would take them to work with him in the field the following day.
4. Because it was a lie; there was no man who sold bread.
5. Because he was starving and tired.

Multiple Choice

1. d)
2. a)
3. c)
4. c)
5. d)

Chapter 5 – O Grande Castanheiro

Numa **aldeia** remota em Trás-os-Montes, longe de tudo e de todos, havia um grande castanheiro, que era o único dessa aldeia. Este castanheiro era muito admirado e adorado por todos os habitantes da aldeia. Em primeiro lugar, pelo seu tamanho. Os habitantes da aldeia, mesmo os que já tinham viajado por outras terras, nunca tinham visto uma árvore tão grande. Os **ramos** estendiam-se por metros, e o tronco era muito, muito grosso e alto.

In a remote village in Trás-os-Montes, far from everything and everyone, there was a great chestnut tree, which was the only one in that village. This chestnut tree was very admired and adored by all of the inhabitants of the village. First of all, due to its size. The inhabitants of the village, even those who had already traveled to other villages, had never seen such a large tree. The branches were several meters long, and the trunk was very, very thick and tall.

Além de todo o seu **esplendor**, as pessoas também tinham uma grande **estima** pelo castanheiro porque este ajudava os habitantes de várias formas. A madeira que retiravam dos grandes ramos e galhos que iam caindo servia para fazer todo o tipo de **construções**: casas, camas, barracas, utensílios, **mobília** para o interior das casas, ferramentas, etc. Além de servir vários fins, a madeira era ainda de muito boa qualidade, e bastante resistente às temperaturas muito baixas e muito altas, que se sentiam no Inverno e no Verão, **respectivamente**, naquela aldeia.

Besides all of its splendor, people also had great esteem for the chestnut tree because it helped the inhabitants in various ways. The wood that they took from the large branches and twigs that were falling was used to make all kinds of constructions: houses, beds, shacks, utensils, house furniture, tools, etc. Besides serving several purposes, the wood was of incredible quality, and very resistant to very low and very high temperatures, which were felt during the winter and the summer, respectively, in that village.

Mas não só a madeira da árvore era usada pelos habitantes. Também as grandes **folhas** do grande castanheiro eram aproveitadas para fazer roupa, mantas, cobertores, cortinados, toalhas, tapetes, guardanapos, e tantas outras coisas. As folhas eram **suaves**, mas resistentes, e as roupas ou qualquer outro **tecido** feito a partir daquelas folhas durava vários anos. Além disso, como a cor das folhas mudava durante as estações do ano, os habitantes jogavam com isso. Por exemplo, no **Outono**, as folhas estavam avermelhadas, criando uma **tonalidade** muito bonita, enquanto que ma Primavera são verdes.

But the wood was not the only thing used by the inhabitants. The large leaves of the great chestnut tree were also used to make clothes, covers, blankets, curtains, towels, carpets, napkins, and so many other things. The leaves were soft but sturdy, and the clothes or any other fabric made from those leaves lasted for several years. Moreover, since the color of the leaves changed during the different seasons of the year, the inhabitants could take advantage of that. For instance, in the fall, the leaves were reddish, creating a very beautiful hue, while in the spring, they were green.

Porém, não era só a madeira e as folhas que eram usadas. Também as **castanhas**, o fruto do castanheiro era usado pelos habitantes como **fonte** principal de alimentação. A colheita do fruto era feita em Novembro, e havia tantas castanhas, que chegavam para o ano todo. As castanhas podiam ser cozidas, assadas ou fritas, feitas em puré, ou usadas em mil e uma receitas que os locais foram aperfeiçoando ao longo dos anos. Para não se **enjoarem** de castanhas, foram várias as ideias que tiveram para diversificar as suas refeições. Mas as castanhas não serviam só de alimento aos habitantes. Como aquele castanheiro era tão grande, as castanhas que **sobravam** eram usadas também para alimentar os animais, que **adoravam** aquela comida e nunca se **fartavam**.

However, it was not just the wood and the leaves that were used. The chestnuts, the fruit of the chestnut tree, were also used by the inhabitants as the main source of food. The fruit was harvested in November, and there were so many chestnuts, that one harvest lasted for the whole year. The chestnuts could be cooked, roasted or fried, mashed just like mashed potatoes, or used in 1,001 recipes that the locals had perfected over the years. They had a lot of ideas to diversify their meals, just so they wouldn't get sick and tired of chestnuts. But the chestnuts did not serve only as food to the inhabitants. That chestnut tree was so large that the spare chestnuts were also used to feed the animals, who loved that dish and never had enough of it.

Ainda assim, não era só a madeira, nem as folhas, nem as castanhas que os habitantes usavam no seu dia-a-dia. Também as cúpulas espinhosas onde se encontram as castanhas são usadas para muitas coisas. A população usa-as principalmente para fazer **vedações** nas suas casas, mas também para decorar o interior.

Still, it was not just the wood, nor the leaves, nor the chestnuts that the inhabitants used in their day-to-day life. The spiny cupules where the chestnuts are found are used for many things as well. The population uses them mainly to make fences in their homes, but also to decorate the interior.

Era então claro que aquele castanheiro tinha assim muita **utilidade** para os habitantes da aldeia. No entanto, uma **tragédia** estava prestes a acontecer. Um fungo que afectava os castanheiros estava rapidamente a disseminar-se em Portugal. Tinha começado em Espanha, na Galiza, e agora estava a atravessar a **fronteira**. Para **impedir** que se espalhasse, os especialistas recomendavam que se abatesse as árvores infectadas e todas aquelas que estavam próximas.

It was clear that the chestnut tree was very useful to the villagers. However, a tragedy was about to happen. A fungus that affected the chestnut trees was rapidly spreading in Portugal. It had begun spreading in Spain, in Galicia, and now it was crossing the border. To prevent it from spreading, the specialists recommended that the infected trees were cut down, as well as all of those which were too close.

O presidente da freguesia, quando soube daquela notícia, chamou logo os especialistas, para averiguarem se o castanheiro da aldeia estava infectado. E estava mesmo. Depois dos especialistas darem o seu **parecer**, o presidente da freguesia reuniu-se com a população da aldeia, para lhes contar o que estava a acontecer. Todos entenderam imediatamente as consequências daquele problema, e sabiam que só havia uma solução: cortar a árvore.

When the president of the village's parish heard about that, he immediately called the experts, so they could determine whether the village's chestnut tree was infected. And it actually was. The experts gave their opinion, and after that, the president of the village's parish met with the population to tell them what was happening. Everyone immediately understood the consequences of that problem, and they knew there was only one solution: cut down the tree.

Toda a gente ficou triste e **preocupada**. Triste porque adoravam aquela árvore—tinha sido uma companheira e um **marco** daquela aldeia durante muitos anos. Era **esplêndida, majestosa**, e despedirem-se dela ia ser difícil. Mas também estavam preocupados porque dependiam da árvore para sobreviver. Quase tudo o que tinham—desde casas, objectos, roupa, alimentação, originava daquela árvore, das suas folhas e das suas castanhas. Como iam fazer agora para sobreviver? O presidente da freguesia tentou acalmar a população, dizendo que iriam encontrar uma solução para resolver este problema, mas ainda não tinha conseguido encontrar nenhuma.

Everybody was sad and worried. Sad because they loved that tree— it had been a companion and the landmark of that village for so many years. It was splendid, majestic, and to say goodbye to it was going to be difficult. But they were also concerned because they depended on the tree to survive. Almost everything they had—from houses, objects, clothing, food, originated from that tree, from its leaves and its chestnuts. What would they do now to survive? The president of the parish tried to calm the population down, saying that they would find a solution to solve this problem, but he had nothing in mind.

Quando chegou o dia de cortar a árvore, toda a população se reuniu em **redor** dela. Ao verem a árvore cair, alguns até choraram. No entanto, uma mulher reparou que os homens que cortavam a árvore e que punham o tronco já num camião deixaram lá todas as castanhas que estavam no chão. Perguntou:

When the day to cut down the tree came, the whole population gathered around it. When they saw the tree fall down to the ground, some even cried. However, a woman noticed that the men who were cutting down the tree and putting the trunk in a truck left all of the chestnuts that were there on the ground. So, she asked:

– Desculpem, mas as castanhas não estão infectadas também? Não as vão levar?

– Não, as castanhas não são afectadas pelo fungo, só o tronco e as folhas. – respondeu um trabalhador.

– Boa, pelo menos assim ainda temos algumas castanhas durante o resto do ano. Mas quando acabarem estamos perdidos… – disse um homem que estava por perto e tinha ouvido a conversa.

– Não! Não vamos desperdiçar estas castanhas em comida; além disso, temos muitas ainda em **reserva**. O que podemos fazer é plantá-las, a todas, e ficar com tantos castanheiros, que mesmo que alguns fiquem podres, teremos muitos outros de que poderemos depender e assim continuar as nossas vidas! – disse com bastante entusiasmo a mulher.

– Excuse me, but aren't the chestnuts infected as well? Aren't you taking them?

– No, the chestnuts are not affected by the fungus, only the trunk and the leaves. – a worker replied.

– Good, at least we will still have some chestnuts for the rest of the year. But once we are done with those, we are lost... – said a man who was nearby and had heard the conversation.

– No! Let's not waste these chestnuts as food; besides, we have many left. What we can do is plant them, all of them, and grow so many chestnut trees, that even if some rot in the future, we will have many others one which we can rely on and continue our lives! – said the woman enthusiastically.

Quem ouviu o que a senhora tinha dito passou a palavra ao do lado, e assim que toda a gente percebeu qual era a ideia, ouviu-se uma **chuva de palmas**. Foi assim que, mesmo a morrer, a árvore deu ainda à sua população, por uma última vez, o que precisavam para sobreviver.

Whoever heard what the lady had said passed the word to someone else, and when everyone realized what the idea was, a round of applause could be heard. That was how, even when it was dying, the chestnut tree gave its population, one last time, what they needed to survive.

Sumário

Em Trás-os-Montes, numa aldeia remota, havia um grande e velho castanheiro que era admirado por todas as pessoas da aldeia. Esta grande árvore dava castanhas para as pessoas comerem, dava madeira para se construir casas, dava folhas que as pessoas usavam para fazer roupa, e dava uma grande sombra, para quem queria descansar depois de um longo dia de trabalho. A árvore era tão grande que era a única da aldeia, e todas as pessoas da aldeia sobreviviam, de uma forma ou outra, das coisas que a árvore proporcionava. Quando um dia, a árvore começou a apodrecer e teve que ser cortada, os habitantes da aldeia desesperaram. No entanto, mesmo a morrer, a árvore ainda tinha algo para dar...

Summary

In Trás-os-Montes, in a remote village, there was a big and old chestnut tree that was admired by everyone in the village. This big tree gave chestnuts for people to eat, gave wood to build houses, gave leaves that people used to make clothing, and it cast a big shadow, for whoever wanted to rest after a hard day's work. The tree was so big that it was the only one in the village, and everyone survived, in one way or another, from the things the tree provided. When, one day, the tree started rotting and had to be cut down, the villagers despaired. Nevertheless, and even though it was dying, the tree still had something to give...

Vocabulary List

Adoravam – adored, loved, worshipped;

Aldeia – small village;

Castanha – chestnut, but also the color "brown";

Chuva de palmas – literally: "rain of applause";

Construções – constructions, buildings;

Enjoarem – getting sick, nauseated;

Esplêndida – splendid, superb;

Esplendor – splendor;

Estima – esteem, value;

Fartavam – getting tired of something;

Folhas – leafs;

Fronteira – border, limit;

Fungo – fungus;

Impedir – to prevent, to stop;

Majestosa – majestic;

Marco – landmark, and also a name for boys;

Mobília – furniture;

Outono – fall;

Parecer – opinion;

Preocupada – preoccupied, worried;

Ramos – branches, twigs, ramifications;

Redor – around;

Reserva – in stock, but it can also be a "natural reservation" or "table reservation";

Respectivamente – respectively;

Sobravam – left over, spare;

Suaves – soft, smooth;

Tecido – fabric;

Tonalidade – tone, shade, hue;

Tragédia – tragedy;

Utilidade – utility, usefulness, value;

Vedações – fences.

Perguntas

1. Porque admiravam tanto a árvore os habitantes daquela aldeia?
2. O que ameaçava a paz naquela aldeia?
3. Como tinha isso acontecido?
4. Quais eram as consequências desse problema?
5. Como se resolveu a situação?

Escolha Múltipla

1. Quantos castanheiros havia na aldeia?
   a) Dois;
   b) Um;
   c) Três;
   d) Quatro.
2. A madeira era aproveitada para fazer…?
   a) Roupa;
   b) Carros;
   c) Todo o tipo de construções;
   d) Vedações.
3. As folhas eram aproveitadas para fazer…?
   a) Comida;
   b) Papel;
   c) Papel higiénico;
   d) Roupa e tecido.
4. As castanhas eram aproveitadas como…?
   a) Comida;
   b) Brinquedos para as crianças;
   c) Não eram aproveitadas;
   d) Ornamentos para as casas.
5. Quem arranjou a solução para o problema da aldeia?
   a) Uma mulher;
   b) Um homem;
   c) O presidente da freguesia;

d) Os homens que cortavam a árvore.

Questions

1. Why did the locals admire that tree so much?
2. What threatened the peace in the village?
3. How did that happen?
4. What were the consequences of that problem?
5. How was the situation solved?

Multiple Choice

1. How many chestnut trees were there in the village?
   a) Two;
   b) One;
   c) Three;
   d) Four.
2. The wood from the chestnut tree was used to make…?
   a) Clothing;
   b) Cars;
   c) All sorts of constructions;
   d) Fences.
3. The leaves were used as…?
   a) Food;
   b) Paper;
   c) Toilet paper;
   d) Clothing and fabric.
4. The chestnuts were used as…?
   a) Food;
   b) Toys for children;
   c) They weren't used at all;
   d) Home ornaments.
5. Who found the solution to the village's problem?
   a) A woman;
   b) A man;
   c) The president of the village's parish;
   d) The men that were cutting down the three.

Respostas

1. Porque era muito grande e alta, e tinha uma grande utilidade para os habitantes.
2. Um fungo que infectou a grande árvore.
3. Começou em Espanha, na Galiza, e espalhou-se até Portugal.
4. Iriam ter que cortar o castanheiro, e isso significava que iam perder a árvore que lhes dava tantas coisas.
5. Plantaram-se as castanhas, que não estavam infectadas, e assim iriam ter muitos castanheiros no futuro.

Escolha Múltipla

1. b)
2. c)
3. d)
4. a)
5. a)

Answers

1. Because it was very wide and tall, and the locals used it for several things.
2. A fungus infected the tree.
3. It started in Spain, in Galicia, and then spread to Portugal.
4. They would have to cut down the chestnut tree, and that meant they would lose the tree that gave them so many things.
5. The chestnuts, which did not get infected, were planted, and this way they would have many chestnut trees in the future.

Multiple Choice

1. b)
2. c)
3. d)
4. a)
5. a)

Chapter 6 – Vestir-se Para a Ocasião

– Carlos, porque vieste para o jantar com essa roupa? Eu avisei-te que ia estar muito calor aqui! – disse Joana.

– Carlos, why did you come to dinner with that outfit? I warned you it would be very hot in here! – said Joana.

Carlos estava a **suar em bica**. Tinha vestido um **fato** cinzento com uma camisa branca e uma **gravata** azul. Estava todo **aperaltado**, mas insistia com Joana, a **namorada**, que estava bem. O **casal** de namorados ia jantar à casa dos pais de Joana, que ficava numa quinta no interior. No Verão, o calor que fazia era absolutamente **insuportável**. Em Lisboa, a **brisa** do mar ajuda nos dias mais difíceis, mas no interior, não há mar, logo também não há brisa. Joana tinha avisado Carlos para isso, mas Carlos ainda assim vestiu um fato.

Carlos was sweating a lot. He was wearing a gray suit with a white shirt and a blue tie. He was all dressed up, but he kept telling Joana, his girlfriend, that he was fine. The couple was going to have dinner at Joana's parents' house, which was on a farm in the countryside. In the summer, the heat there was absolutely unbearable. In Lisbon, the sea breeze helped during the hardest days, but in the countryside, there is no sea, so there is no breeze. Joana had warned Carlos about this, but Carlos wore a suit anyway.

– Vamos jantar com os teus pais; quero ir bem vestido! – respondeu Carlos.

– Mas já lá fomos tantas vezes. Porque é que hoje decidiste ir assim? – perguntou Joana.

– Acho que é importante fazer um esforço; quero que eles gostem de mim! – **argumentou** Carlos.

– Mas eles já gostam de ti… – respondeu Joana, sem perceber.

– We are going to have dinner with your parents; I want to dress appropriately! – replied Carlos.

– But we've been there so many times. Why did you decide to go like this today? – asked Joana.

– I think it's important to make an effort; I want them to like me! – argued Carlos.

– But they already like you... – replied Joana, not understanding his reasoning.

Entretanto, ainda em viagem no carro, Carlos suava por todos os lados. Nem com **ar condicionado** ou janela aberta a temperatura melhorou. Quando chegaram, e Carlos saiu do carro, parecia que tinham acabado de lhe deitar um balde de água para cima.

Meanwhile, inside the car on their way there, Carlos was sweating even more. The air conditioning or an open window didn't help at all with the temperature. When they arrived, and Carlos got out of the car, he looked like somebody had just thrown a bucket of water on him.

– Carlos, querias vir bem vestido para o jantar, mas neste momento, estás uma **lástima**. Ainda temos tempo antes do jantar, por isso vamos ali ao centro comprar qualquer coisa para tu vestires! – sugeriu Joana.

– Carlos, you wanted to come all dressed up for dinner, but right now, you're a mess. We still have time before dinner, so let's go to the town center to buy something for you to wear! – suggested Joana.

Carlos ainda tentou dizer que estava bem, que não era preciso, que com o calor ia **secar** rapidamente, mas Joana insistiu e Carlos teve que ceder. Além disso, quando se viu ao espelho, viu que não estava mesmo **apresentável**. Então, lá foram eles comprar roupa. No entanto, no centro só havia **lojas** de roupa **casual**. Nem uma camisa decente conseguiram encontrar. Carlos foi a todas as lojas mas teve que se contentar com uma t-shirt e uns **calções**.

Carlos still tried to say that he was fine, that it was not necessary, that with the heat he would dry out quickly, but Joana insisted, and Carlos had to give in. Besides, when he saw himself in the mirror, he realized he really wasn't presentable. So, there they went to buy clothes. However, in the town center, there were only casual clothing stores. He couldn't even find a decent shirt. Carlos went to all the stores but had to settle for a T-shirt and shorts.

– Deixa lá Carlos, é um jantar casual, não é uma **gala**! Não vai fazer diferença nenhuma! – disse Joana.

– Just leave it, Carlos, it's a casual dinner, not a gala! It won't make any difference! – said Joana.

Finalmente, chegou a hora de jantar, e o casal lá foi para a casa dos pais de Joana. O jantar correu lindamente, e a refeição estava deliciosa. Depois, estavam a ir para o jardim para tomar os cafés e beber um copo de **vinho do Porto**, já que fazia uma noite muito **agradável**, quando Carlos pediu a palavra. A sua expressão era **grave** e **séria**, e parecia nervoso. Todos se calaram, curiosos, e um pouco preocupados com o que Carlos iria dizer.

Finally, it was time for dinner, and the couple headed to Joana's parents' house. The dinner went beautifully, and the meal was delicious. After, they were going to the garden to drink the coffees and have a glass of port wine, since it was a very pleasant evening, when Carlos asked to speak. His expression was serious and grave, and he seemed nervous. Everybody stopped talking, curious, and a little worried about what Carlos had to say.

– Joana, estamos juntos há cinco anos. Gosto de tudo acerca de ti. Estou mais seguro do que nunca de que quero passar a minha vida contigo! Queres casar comigo? – disse Carlos, **ajoelhando-se** e tirando um anel do seu bolso.

– Já percebi tudo! Por isso insististe tanto para vir de fato hoje! – disse Joana, com um sorriso gigante.

– Isso é um sim ou um não? – perguntou Carlos, ainda ansioso.

– É um sim, claro que sim! – respondeu Joana, abraçando Carlos.

– Senhor Nuno, Dona Lena, dão-me a vossa **bênção** para casar com a vossa filha? – perguntou Carlos.

– Joana, we've been together for five years. I like everything about you. I have never been so sure that I want to spend my life with you! Will you marry me? – said Carlos, kneeling down and taking a ring out of his pocket.

– I've got it all figured out! This is why you insisted so much in wearing a suit today! – said Joana, with a giant smile.

– Is that a yes or a no? – asked Carlos, still anxious.

– It's a yes, of course! – replied Joana, hugging Carlos.

– Mr. Nuno, Mrs. Lena, will you give me your blessing to marry your daughter? – asked Carlos.

Os pais de Joana, apenas acenaram que sim com a cabeça, enquanto limpavam as lágrimas dos olhos.

Joana's parents just nodded yes with their heads, while wiping the tears from their eyes.

Sumário

Um casal de namorados, Joana e Carlos, vai jantar a casa dos pais de Joana. Estes viviam numa grande quinta no interior do país. No Verão, o calor que lá fazia era insuportável. Embora a sua namorada o tivesse avisado para isso, Carlos achava que estava a exagerar. Assim sendo, não se vestiu com roupa nada fresca, e o resultado não foi surpreendente. No entanto, o casal tentou resolver o assunto, comprando roupas mais frescas, só que nada do que encontraram era apropriado para a refeição, segundo Carlos.

Summary

A couple, Joana and Carlos, is going to have dinner at Joana's parents' house. These two lived in a big manor in the countryside. During the summer, the heat was unbearable. Even though his girlfriend had warned him about that, Carlos thought she was exaggerating. So, he didn't wear light clothes, and the result was not surprising. The couple did, however, try to solve the situation, buying lighter clothes, but nothing they found was appropriate for the meal, according to Carlos…

Vocabulary List

Agradável – nice, pleasant, enjoyable;

Ajoelhando-se – taking a knee, kneeling;

Aperaltado – very nicely dressed or even overdressed;

Apresentável – presentable;

Ar condicionado – air conditioning (AC);

Argumentou – argued;

Benção – blessing;

Brisa – breeze, wind;

Calções – shorts;

Casal – a couple (romantic relationship);

Casual – casual, informal, laidback;

Fato – suit;

Gala – gala;

Gravata – tie;

Grave – grave[18], significant, serious;

Insuportável – unbearable, intolerable;

Lástima – pity,

Lojas – stores, shops;

Namorada – girlfriend (boyfriend = namorado);

Secar – to dry up or out;

Séria – serious, grave;

---

[18] The word "grave" can also be used in a cemetery or graveyard context. The correspondent word in Portuguese is "campa" or "túmulo".

Suar em bica – Portuguese expression, meaning "to sweat a lot";

Vestir-se para ocasião – dress up for the occasion;

Vinho do Porto – Port wine;

Perguntas

1. Porque queria Carlos ir de fato jantar a casa dos pais da namorada?
2. O que aconteceu por estar de fato?
3. Que solução propôs Joana?
4. Depois de jantar, o que foram todos beber? E onde?
5. O que disseram os pais de Joana quando Carlos lhes pediu a mão da filha?

Escolha Múltipla

1. Carlos disse que queria ir bem vestido porque…?
   a) Ia pedir Joana em casamento;
   b) Se vestia assim todos os dias;
   c) Era a primeira vez que ia conhecer os pais de Joana;
   d) Porque queria os pais de Joana gostassem dele.
2. Quando chegaram à casa dos pais de Joana, parecia que tinham atirado cima de Carlos um…?
   a) Saco de terra;
   b) Balde de areia;
   c) Saco de água;
   d) Balde de água.
3. O que comprou Carlos na loja?
   a) Outro fato;
   b) Uma camisa e uns calções;
   c) Uma t-shirt e uns calções;
   d) Uma t-shirt e umas calças.
4. Joana disse que o jantar era…?
   a) Formal;
   b) De gala;
   c) Casual;
   d) Elegante.
5. Porque ficou ansioso Carlos depois de fazer a pergunta?
   a) Joana disse que não;

b) Joana não respondeu logo que sim;

c) Joana começou a chorar;

d) Porque se arrependeu.

Questions

1. Why did Carlos want to wear a suit to dinner at Joana's parents' house?
2. What happened because he was wearing a suit?
3. What solution did Joana suggest?
4. After dinner, what did they all drink? And where?
5. What did Joana's parents say when Carlos asked for their daughter's hand?

Multiple Choice

1. Carlos said he wanted to dress up because…?
   a) He was going to propose;
   b) He dressed like that every day;
   c) It was the first time he was going to meet Joana's parents;
   d) Because he wanted Joana's parents to like him.
2. When they got to Joana's parents' house, it seemed like somebody just threw on Carlos a…?
   a) Bag of dirt;
   b) Bucket of sand;
   c) Bag of water;
   d) Bucket of water.
3. What did Carlos buy at the store?
   a) Another suit;
   b) A shirt and shorts;
   c) A T-shirt and shorts;
   d) A T-shirt and pants.
4. Joana said that the dinner was…?
   a) Formal;
   b) A gala;
   c) Casual;
   d) Elegant.

5. Why was Carlos still anxious after popping the question?
   a) Because Joana said no;
   b) Because Joana didn't answer immediately;
   c) Because Joana started crying;
   d) Because he regretted it.

Respostas

1. Porque ia pedir a namorada em casamento.
2. Começou a suar muito, porque estava muito calor.
3. Propôs que fossem comprar roupa mais leve e fresca ao centro.
4. Foram beber café e um copo de vinho do Porto, no jardim.
5. Nada. Apenas acenaram com a cabeça, porque estavam emocionados.

Escolha Múltipla

1. d)
2. d)
3. c)
4. c)
5. b)

Answers

1. Because he was going to ask his girlfriend to marry him.
2. He started sweating a lot.
3. She suggested that they went to the town's center to buy lighter clothing.
4. Coffee and a glass of Port wine in the garden.
5. Nothing. They just nodded because they were very emotional.

Multiple Choice

1. d)
2. d)
3. c)

4. c)
5. b)

Chapter 7 – Querido Avô

Querido, avô,

Dear, Grandpa,

Há muito tempo que ando a pensar responder-te, mas ainda não tinha arranjado tempo para o fazer. Sei que esta é uma **desculpa** má, mas pelo menos serve de **justificação**. O **trabalho** deixa-me sem tempo para nada, e o bebé chora toda a noite. Não tem sido nada fácil e estou sempre cansada, mas estou a adorar esta nova fase da minha vida.

Não sei se sabes, mas para **além** de eu ser sócia na minha firma de advogados, o David também foi feito sócio recentemente—há cerca de 2 meses. É **incrível**, **claro**, e ele está contentíssimo, mas deixa-nos ainda menos tempo para lidar com o pequeno Daniel. De qualquer forma, o David tem sido **incansável**, e ajuda-me bastante. Como tu disseste a primeira vez o viste—ele vai ser um marido incrível. E é mesmo. O engraçado é que ele diz que o Daniel vai ser como avô, **maluco** pelo futebol porque está sempre a dar **pontapés**. Eu acho que não; para mim, vai ser mais como a avó, **rabugento**, porque está sempre a resmungar e a chorar por alguma coisa!

I've been thinking about writing you back for a long time, but I haven't had the time to do it. I know this is a bad excuse, but at least it's an explanation. The job leaves me with no time for anything, and the baby cries all night. It hasn't been easy and I'm always tired, but I'm loving this new moment of my life.

I don't know if you know, but besides me being a partner in my law firm, David was also made a partner recently—about two months ago. It's amazing, of course, and he's very happy, but it leaves us with even less time to deal with little Daniel. Anyway, David has been tireless, and he helps me a lot. Like you said the first time you saw him—he's going to be an amazing husband. And he really is. Funny thing is he says Daniel's going to be like Grandpa, a crazy soccer fan because he is always kicking. I don't agree; for me, he is going to be more like Grandma, grumpy, because he is always mumbling and crying for something!

Mas agora mais a sério, estamos muito felizes com este momento das nossas vidas.

Escrevo-te também para te contar o que me aconteceu noutro dia. Estava no supermercado a comprar alguns vegetais e fruta, mas como já era o final do dia, já não se conseguia encontrar nada de **jeito**. Encontrei uma curgete bem pequenina, as beringelas estavam todas comidas por bichos, e não encontrei nem um pepino. Quanto à fruta ainda pior. Havia muitas peças de frutas—mas estavam todas

podres. Via **nitidamente** os buracos na **superfície**. Foi então que ao me **deparar** com isto, disse em voz alta, "Isto está cheio de minhocas!" Não tinha **reparado**, mas estava uma senhora velhota ao meu lado. Ela riu-se quando eu disse isto, e depois disse-me, "Sabe o que é pior que dar uma **trinca** numa fruta e ver uma minhoca lá dentro?" E eu disse que não sabia, mas aquela pergunta não me era nada estranha. E ela continuou: "Dar uma trinca numa fruta, e ver **metade** de uma minhoca lá dentro!" E finalmente lembrei-me: era a avó Nena que dizia isto! Quase que comecei a chorar no meio do supermercado, com aquela **memória inesperada**. Foi uma pequena história que fez lembrar a avó e que me **aqueceu** o coração. Tenho tantas **saudades** dela! **Enfim**...Espero que esteja tudo bem aí pelo Norte e que o Pai te esteja a tratar bem—não o deixes pôr muito sal na comida!

But now, in all seriousness, we are very happy with this moment of our lives.

I'm also writing to tell you what happened to me the other day. I was at the grocery store buying some vegetables and fruit, but since it was the end of the day, there was no way to find anything good and fresh. I found a very tiny zucchini, the eggplants were all eaten by bugs, and I couldn't find one cucumber. As for the fruit, even worse. There were many pieces of fruit—but they were all rotten. I clearly saw the holes on the surface. It was when I came across this that I said aloud, "This is full of worms!" I hadn't noticed, but there was an old lady next to me. She laughed when I said it, and then she said to me, "You know what's worse than taking a bite out of a fruit and seeing a worm inside?" And I said I didn't know, but that question seemed familiar. And she went on, "Take a bite out of a fruit, and see half a worm in there!" And finally, I remembered: it was Grandma Nena who said that! I almost started crying in the middle of the supermarket with that unexpected memory. It was a little story that reminded me of Grandma and warmed my heart. I miss her so much!

Anyway... I hope everything is well over there in the North, and that Dad is taking care of you—don't let him put a lot of salt in the food!

Eu e o David gostávamos que nos viesses visitar **um dia destes**. Nós vamos-te buscar, ficas cá uns dias, e depois levamos-te de volta—é só dizeres quando podes.

Espero ouvir de ti em **breve**! E, avô... **gosto muito de ti**!

David and I would really like that you visit us sometime. We will pick you up, you stay here for a few days, and then we'll take you back—you just have to tell us when you can do that.

Hoping to hear from you soon! And, Grandpa... I love you very much!

Com muito amor,

Much love,

A tua neta, Lurdes

Your granddaughter, Lurdes

Sumário

Uma neta escreve uma carta ao seu avô para lhe contar como vai a sua vida. Lurdes trabalha numa firma de advogados, tal como o seu marido, e tiveram um bebé recentemente. O trabalho que estão a ter na firma mais as noites sem dormir por causa do seu filho Daniel, estão a deixá-los aos dois muito cansados. Apesar disso, estão os dois muito contentes com esta nova fase da vida deles. Ainda assim, e apesar da felicidade que vive, há um momento banal que deixa Lurdes um pouco nostálgica...

Summary

A granddaughter writes a letter to her grandfather to tell him how her life is going. Lurdes works at a law firm, just like her husband, and they had a baby recently. The work they're having at the firm plus the sleepless nights because of their son Daniel is leaving them both very tired. Nevertheless, they are both very happy with this new moment in their lives. Still, and despite the happiness she is living, there is a casual moment that leaves Lurdes somewhat nostalgic...

Vocabulary List

Além – when "disso" goes after it means "besides", but without it means "over there";

Aqueceu – warmed;

Breve – brief. "Em breve" means soon.

Claro – clear (as water), but it can also mean "obviously";

Deparar – came across, run into;

Desculpa – excuse, but it can also mean "I'm sorry";

Enfim – anyway, whatever;

Gosto muito de ti – literally: "I like you a lot" but it means "I love you a lot". "I love you" – "eu amo-te", is more commonly used in a romantic relationship;

Incansável – tireless, relentless;

Incrível – incredible, amazing;

Inesperada – unexpected;

Jeito – style, way, manner, but also "being good at something" – "ter jeito para algo";

Justificação – justification, explanation;

Maluco – crazy, mad, lunatic;

Memória – memory;

Metade – half;

Nitidamente – distinctly, clearly;

Podres – bad, rotten;

Pontapés – kicks;

Rabugenta – cranky, grumpy, moody;

Reparado – noticed, but also "fixed", "repaired";

Saudades – no word in English corresponds to this one, but it means "to miss someone or something";

Superfície – surface;

Trabalho – work, job:

Trinca – bite;

Um dia destes – literally: "one of these days", meaning "soon".

Perguntas

1. Porque é a neta demorou tanto para responder ao avô?
2. Qual é a profissão dela e do marido?
3. Quem é o Daniel?
4. Uma senhora falou com a Lurdes no supermercado. A conversa fê-la lembrar quem?
5. O que propõe a Lurdes ao avô?

Escolha Múltipla

1. David acha que o filho Daniel vai ser jogador de futebol. Porquê?
   a) Porque está sempre a brincar com uma bola;
   b) Porque está sempre a dar pontapés;
   c) Porque está sempre a fazer fitas;
   d) Porque gosta muito de futebol.
2. O que foi Lurdes comprar ao supermercado?
   a) Doces;
   b) Vegetais e fruta;
   c) Batatas fritas;
   d) Arroz e massa.
3. De que vegetal não havia nem sequer uma peça?
   a) Pepino;
   b) Abóbora;
   c) Beringela;
   d) Curgete.
4. O que tinham as frutas por dentro?
   a) Minhocas;
   b) Bichos;
   c) Moscas;
   d) Mosquitos da fruta.
5. Lurdes espera que o pai esteja a tratar bem o avô. O que é que ela diz ao avô que não pode deixar o pai fazer?
   a) Comer fritos;

b) Trabalhar muito;

c) Pôr demasiado sal na comida;

d) Dormir pouco.

Questions

1. Why did the granddaughter take so long to answer back?
2. What is both her and her husband's profession?
3. Who is Daniel?
4. A lady talked to Lurdes in the supermarket. Her conversation reminded her of whom?
5. What does Lurdes propose to her grandfather?

Multiple Choice

1. David thinks his son Daniel will be a soccer player. Why?
   a) Because he is always playing with a ball;
   b) Because he is always kicking;
   c) Because he is always making tantrums;
   d) Because he likes soccer a lot.

2. Lurdes went to the supermarket to buy what?
   a) Candy;
   b) Vegetables and fruit;
   c) Chips;
   d) Rice and pasta.

3. Of which vegetable wasn't a piece left?
   a) Cucumber;
   b) Pumpkin;
   c) Eggplant;
   d) Zucchini.

4. What was inside the fruit?
   a) Worms;
   b) Bugs;
   c) Flies;
   d) Fruit flies.

5. Lurdes hopes her dad is taking good care of her grandfather. What does she tell her grandfather that he mustn't let his son do?

a) Eat fried food;

b) Work a lot;

c) Put a lot of salt in the food;

d) Sleep very little.

Respostas

1. Porque estava muito ocupada.
2. São advogados.
3. O Daniel é o filho dela, bebé recém-nascido.
4. Fê-la lembrar da avó.
5. Que o avô venha passar uns dias à casa de Lurdes e David.

Escolha Múltipla

1. b)
2. b)
3. a)
4. a)
5. c)

Answers

1. Because she was really busy.
2. They are lawyers.
3. Daniel is her newborn baby.
4. It reminded her of her grandmother.
5. That he comes to visit for a few days.

Multiple Choice

1. b)
2. b)
3. a)
4. a)
5. c)

Chapter 8 – O Clube Real dos Saltadores

Beatriz e Leonor são duas rãs que vão iniciar uma longa viagem para ir conhecer o Rei Sapo. Nunca o tinham **conhecido** ou visto antes já que ele vivia numa terra muito longe, mais ou menos a 1,500 saltos de distância.

Beatriz and Leonor are two toads that will start a long journey to meet the Frog King. They had never seen or meet him before since he lived in a faraway land, more or less 1,500 hops away.

– **Bom dia alegria**! – disse Beatriz, assim que saltou da cama.

– Bom dia, Beatriz! Acordaste muito bem-disposta hoje! – disse-lhe Leonor.

– Claro! É o dia em que começamos a nossa viagem! – respondeu Beatriz.

– Good morning joy! – said Beatriz, as she jumped out of bed.

– Good morning, Beatriz! You're in a very good mood today! – said Leonor.

– Of course! Today is the day we start our trip! – answered Beatriz.

Então, depois do pequeno-almoço, puseram a mochila às costas, e começaram a saltar para a terra do Rei. Ao chegar perto da hora de almoço, decidiram entrar numa pequena **vila** para comerem bem num restaurante. Entraram no primeiro restaurante que encontraram porque estavam **cheias de fome.** Estava cheio de animais diferentes, como cavalos, mosquitos, cães e corujas. Enquanto estavam sentados à espera da comida que tinham pedido, uma pulga que estava na mesa ao lado da mesa delas, começou a falar. Disse:

So, after breakfast, with a backpack, they started hopping away towards the King's land. When it was almost lunchtime, they decided to go to a small village to eat well at a restaurant. They went in the first restaurant they could find because they were starving. It was full of different animals, such as horses, mosquitoes, dogs, and owls. While they were waiting for the food they had ordered, a flea that was on the table beside their table, started talking to them. It said:

– Vocês não são daqui, pois não?

– Não, somos de outra terra, não muito longe daqui – uns meros 200 saltos de distância. – respondeu Leonor.

– Bem me parecia. Almoço aqui todos os dias, e não vos **reconhecia**. E eu conheço quase toda a gente. – acrescentou a pulga.
– E para onde se dirigem, se não se importam de partilhar?

– Vamos para a terra do Rei! – disse prontamente Beatriz. – Vamos vê-lo pela primeira vez.

– Não me digam! Também eu vou para lá depois de almoço. Não acredito que vão também participar no concurso das boas acções! – disse com entusiasmo a pulga.

– You're not from around here, are you?

– No, we're from another land, not very far away from here – a mere 200 hops away. – answered Leonor.

– I thought so. I have lunch here every day, and I didn't recognize you guys. And I know almost everybody. – added the flea. – And where are you headed to, if you don't mind sharing?

– We're headed to the King's land! – said Beatriz immediately. – We are going to see him for the first time.

– Shut up! I'm also headed there after lunch. I can't believe you will also participate in the good deeds contest! – said the flea enthusiastically.

As rãs não faziam a **mínima ideia** do que estava a falar a pulga. Beatriz perguntou então de que concurso de tratava, e a pulga simplesmente **apontou**, com o dedo indicador, para um cartaz colado na **janela** perto deles. Dizia: "O Rei Sapo anuncia a abertura do concurso anual de boas acções. O animal que fizer a melhor acção até domingo, será membro da **Clube Real** dos Saltadores, com direito a todos os privilégios associados."

The toads had no idea what the flea was talking about. Beatriz then asked what contest it was, and the flea simply pointed, with its index finger, to a poster that was up in a window nearby. It said: "The Frog

King announces the opening of the annual contest of good deeds. Whichever animal does the best deed until Sunday will be made a member of the Royal Club of Jumpers, with granted right to all of its associated privileges."

– Eu quero fazer **parte** do Clube Real de Saltadores! – disse Leonor. – Assim vou poder passar a nadar no lago do **palácio**.

– Eu também quero ser! Assim poderei apanhar sol na **varanda** do palácio. – acrescentou a Beatriz.

– I want to be a part of the Royal Club of Jumpers! – said Leonor. – Then I'll be allowed to swim in the palace's pond.

– Me too! Then I could take sunbaths in the palace's balcony. – added Beatriz.

Os três decidiram então começar a sua viagem. Ainda ia demorar um pouco para lá chegar, e queriam chegar lá antes da hora de jantar. A meio da tarde, chegaram a outra terra que não era muito longe da terra do Rei. Na verdade, a terra do Rei era logo a seguir ao rio. Enquanto tentavam encontrar alguém para pedir direcções para a ponte, conheceram uma cabra velha com uma longa barba branca. Perguntaram-lhe onde era a ponte, mas a cabra surpreendeu-os:

The three then decided to start their journey. It would still take a while to get there, and they wanted to arrive before dinnertime. In the middle of the afternoon, they reached another village that wasn't that far away from the King's land. Actually, the King's land was just past the village's river. While trying to find anyone to ask for directions to the bridge, they met an old goat with a long white beard. They asked him where the bridge was, but the goat surprised them:

– Vocês não vão conseguir atravessar a ponte... - disse a velha cabra.

– Porquê? – perguntou logo a pulga.

– Porque a ponte foi destruída pelas chuvas **fortes** o último Inverno e ainda ninguém a **reconstruiu**. – explicou a cabra.

– Então como fazemos agora para ir para a terra do Rei? – perguntou preocupada Beatriz.

– Têm que ir dar a volta. São mais 20.000 saltos de viagem. Podem ficar cá durante a noite, se quiserem. – acrescentou a cabra.

– You won't be able to cross the bridge… – said the old goat.

– Why not? – asked the flea immediately.

– Because the bridge has been destroyed by the heavy rains last winter and nobody has yet reconstructed it. – explained the goat.

– Then how will we get to the King's land? – asked Beatriz, worried.

– You will have to go around. It is more than 20,000 hops. You can stay here for the night, if you want. – added the goat.

– Oh não! De certeza que iríamos **perder** a oportunidade de estar no concurso… E se nadássemos para atravessar o rio? – propôs Beatriz.

– Eu acho que devíamos ficar aqui e ajudar os animais desta terra. Temos que reconstruir a ponte por eles. – disse Leonor.

– Sim, eu concordo… É tão **injusto** para eles. – disse Beatriz.

–Bem, vocês podem fazer o que quiserem, mas eu vou nadar até ao outro lado. Não vou perder a chance de estar no Clube Real! – respondeu a pulga, de forma **rude**.

– Oh no! We would for sure miss the chance to be in the contest... What if we just swim across? – proposed Beatriz.

– I think we must stay here and help the animals from this land. We must rebuild the bridge for them. – said Leonor.

– Yes, I agree... It is so unfair for them. – said Beatriz.

– Well, you can do what you like, but I'm swimming across. I won't miss the chance to be in the Royal Club! – replied the flea, rudely.

E depois a pulga foi-se embora. Saltou para as costas de um crocodilo e atravessou o rio. As duas rãs, Leonor e Beatriz, estavam um pouco tristes já que tinham feito este caminho todo para nada. Mas o sentimento de que estavam a fazer a coisa certa fê-las sentir melhor. Decidiram que iriam ficar lá durante a noite, e começar a trabalhar na ponte na manhã seguinte.

And then the flea left. It jumped to the back of a crocodile and crossed the river. The two toads, Leonor and Beatriz, were a bit sad since they came all this way for nothing. But the feeling that they were doing the right thing made them feel better. They decided they would stay there during the night, and start working on the bridge the next morning.

Na manhã seguinte, Beatriz e Leonor começaram a trabalhar. Demoraram o dia todo a arranjar a ponte. Enquanto o estavam a fazer, não conseguiam não pensar no que a pulga estaria a fazer naquele momento, e onde estaria. No palácio, talvez?

The next morning Beatriz and Leonor got to work. It took them the whole day to fix the broken bridge. While they were doing it, they couldn't help but think of what the flea was doing at that moment, and where would it be. The palace, perhaps?

Quando a ponte estava terminada, na manhã seguinte a terem começado a **arranjá-la**, todos os animais da cidade puderam **atravessar** em segurança o rio. Era meio da tarde quando Beatriz e Leonor finalmente chegar à terra do Rei. Dirigiram-se à praça da vila para ver quem tinha sido o vencedor do concurso já que era domingo. Quando lá chegaram, viram o Rei na varanda. Que vista incrível! Ele começou então a falar para o **resto** dos animais:

When the bridge was finished, the morning after they started fixing it, all the animals in that village were able to safely cross the river. It was the middle of the afternoon when Beatriz and Leonor finally reached the King's land. They headed to the town's square to see who the winner of the contest was since it was Sunday. When they got there, they saw the King on the balcony. What an incredible sight! He then started talking to the rest of the animals:

– Como anunciado, hoje seria o último dia para participar no concurso das boas acções. Houve muitas boas acções ao longo desta semana, e até tínhamos já um vencedor escolhido, antes de eventos recentes terem chegado às minhas **ouvidos** – disse o Rei, a sorrir. Depois, continuou – Podem os animais da terra do outro lado do rio apontar para os bons animais que preferiram fazer uma boa acção, do que deixar os outros sozinhos, em busca de sonhos de **glória** e luxo, por favor?

– As announced, today would be the last day to participate in the contest of good deeds. There were a lot of good deeds throughout the last week, and we even had a winner, before recent events came to my attention. – said the King, smiling. He then continued – Can the animals from the village across the river point to the good animals that preferred doing a good deed than leaving others alone by going after dreams of glory and luxury, please?

E assim que o Rei Sapo disse isto, todos os animais apontaram para Beatriz e Leonor. O Rei concluiu:

And as the Frog King said this, every animal pointed to Beatriz and Leonor. The King then concluded:

– **Parabéns,** Beatriz e Leonor, pela vossa incrível boa acção. A partir de agora, vocês são ambas membros do Clube Real de Saltadores.

– Congratulations, Beatriz and Leonor, for your incredibly good deed. From now on, you both are members of the Royal Club of Jumpers!

Sumário

Um par de rãs dirigia-se para a terra do Rei para conhecer o Rei Sapo pela primeira vez. Durante o caminho, pararam numa terra para almoçar. Lá, elas conheceram uma pulga que também se encaminhava para a terra do Rei para participar num concurso. As rãs não sabiam nada sobre o concurso, mas quando souberam sobre o que era e qual era a recompensa por ganhar, ficar logo muito interessadas. Os três decidiram então fazer o resto da viagem juntos. Mais tarde, chegaram a uma vila perto da terra do Rei. Mas havia um problema que os impediu de chegar ao seu destino final. No entanto, o que parecia um obstáculo nas suas vidas, acabou por se tornar precisamente naquilo que precisavam...

Summary

A couple of frogs was headed to the King's land to meet the Frog King for the first time. Along the way, they stopped in a village for lunch. There, they met a flea that was headed towards the King's land as well to participate in a contest. The frogs didn't know anything about this contest, but once they knew what it was about and what the reward for winning was, they were very interested. The three decided to make the rest of the trip together. Later that day, they reached a village near the King's land. But there was a problem that prevented them from reaching their final destination. However, what seemed an obstacle in their life, actually proved to be the exact thing they needed...

Vocabulary List

Apontou – pointed, pointed out;

Arranjá-la – fixing it, mending it;

Atravessar – pass through, cross;

Bom dia alegria – literally: "good morning joy", it is common phrase to say in the morning because it rhymes;

Cheios de fome – literally: "full of hunger", it means "starving";

Clube real – royal club. "Real" can also mean "real", depending on the context;

Conhecido – met, but also "known";

Fortes – strong, but it can be used to nicely describe someone who is fat;

Glória – glory;

Injusto – unfair;

Janela – window;

Mínima ideia – no clue, no idea, but literally, "minimal idea";

Ouvidos – ears;

Palácio – palace;

Parabéns – congratulations, but it is also used to wish a happy birthday;

Parte – a bit of something, being part of something, breaking something, from the verb "partir", which can also mean "to leave", as well as "to break";

Perder – to lose;

Reconhecia – recognized;

Reconstruiu – rebuilt, reconstructed;

Resto – (the) rest, remains, leftovers;

Rude – rude, unkind;

Varanda – balcony;

Vila – village.

Perguntas

1. Porque iniciam a viagem Beatriz e Leonor?
2. Porque se junta a elas uma pulga?
3. Qual era o prémio por ganhar o concurso?
4. Que decidiram fazer as rãs quando souberam que a ponte estava destruída?
5. Porque ganharam as rãs o concurso?

Escolha Múltipla

1. A que distância ficava a terra do Rei de onde viviam as rãs?
   a) 3,000 saltos de distância;
   b) 2,000 saltos de distância;
   c) 1,500 saltos de distância;
   d) 2,500 saltos de distância.
2. Porque entraram Beatriz e Leonor na pequena vila?
   a) Porque se perderam;
   b) Porque era a terra do rei;
   c) Porque estavam esfomeadas e queriam comer;
   d) Porque iam encontrar-se com a pulga.
3. Porque queria Leonor ganhar o concurso?
   a) Porque queria apanhar sol na varanda;
   b) Porque queria a fama e a glória;
   c) Porque queria conhecer o Rei Sapo;
   d) Porque queria nadar no lago do palácio.
4. Porque queria Beatriz ganhar o concurso?
   a) Porque queria apanhar sol na varanda;
   b) Porque queria a fama e a glória;

c) Porque queria conhecer o Rei Sapo;

d) Porque queria nadar no lago do palácio.

5. A pulga atravessou o rio para ir para a terra do Rei. Como?

a) A nadar;

b) Às costas de um crocodilo;

c) A saltar;

d) Pela ponte.

Questions

1. Why are Beatriz and Leonor going on a trip?
2. Why does a flea join them?
3. What was the prize for winning the contest?
4. What did the toads decide to do once they heard about the destroyed bridge?
5. Why did the toads win the contest?

Multiple Choice

1. How far away was the King's land from where the toads lived?

a) 3,000 hops away;

b) 2,000 hops away;

c) 1,500 hops away;

d) 2,500 hops away.

2. Why did Beatriz and Leonor go in that small village?

a) Because they were lost;

b) Because it was the King's land;

c) Because they were starving, and they wanted to eat;

d) Because they were meeting the flea there.

3. Why did Leonor want to win the contest?

a) Because she wanted to take sunbaths in the palace's balcony;

b) Because she wanted the fame and glory;

c) Because she wanted to meet the Frog King;

d) Because she wanted to swim in the palace's pond.

4. Why did Beatriz want to win the contest?
   a) Because she wanted to take sunbaths in the palace's balcony;
   b) Because she wanted the fame and glory;
   c) Because she wanted to meet the Frog King;
   d) Because she wanted to swim in the palace's pond.
5. The flea crossed the river to go to the King's land. How?
   a) Swimming;
   b) On the back of a crocodile;
   c) Jumping;
   d) By the bridge.

Respostas

1. Porque querem ir ver o Rei Sapo.
2. Porque ia participar num concurso na terra do Rei.
3. O vencedor passa a ser membro do Clube Real de Saltadores.
4. Elas decidiram ficar lá e arranjar a ponte
5. Porque foram elas a fazer a melhor acção.

Escolha Múltipla

1. c)
2. c)
3. d)
4. a)
5. b)

Answers

1. Because they want to go see the Frog King.
2. Because it is going to the King's land to participate in a contest.
3. The winner becomes a member of the Royal Club of Jumpers.
4. They decided to stay there and mend the bridge.
5. Because they were the ones with the best deed.

Multiple Choice

1. c)
2. c)
3. d)
4. a)
5. b)

Chapter 9 – Quando a Saudade Aperta...

O grupo de amigos, Diogo, Miguel, António, e Tiago, estão na Bélgica na primeira semana do **mês** de Dezembro. Os amigos estão a fazer um InterRail pela Europa, e passam uma **semana** em cada país. Estavam muito contentes por estar em Bruges—já que era a cidade que os tinha levado a fazer o InterRail em primeiro lugar. Foi lá que Tiago conheceu o seu primeiro amor, e tinha sido ele também a convencer todos os outros a visitarem a cidade. Depois, acabaram por descobrir que havia um interrail que passava por lá, e rapidamente se decidiram começar essa grande aventura.

The group of friends, Diogo, Miguel, António, and Tiago, are in Belgium in the first week of December. The friends are doing an InterRail across Europe, spending one week in every country. They were very happy to be in Bruges—since it was the city that had led them to do the InterRail in the first place. It was there that Tiago met his first love, and he was also the one that had persuaded everyone else to visit the city. Afterward, they discovered that there was an InterRail that passed by the city, and immediately decided to start that great adventure.

No entanto, já há alguns meses que estavam fora de casa. Tinham iniciado a sua viagem em Janeiro, há quase um ano, e o **ambiente** de

Natal nas ruas de Bruges fê-los lembrar da bonita Avenida da Liberdade em Lisboa, decorada com **luzes** de Natal, das suas casas, e das suas famílias. Miguel, algo **comovido**, deixou escapar um **suspiro**.

However, they had been away from home for a few months now. They had started their trip in January, almost a year before, and the Christmas spirit in the streets of Bruges reminded them of the beautiful Liberdade's Avenue in Lisbon, decorated with Christmas lights, their homes, and their families. Miguel, somewhat moved, sighed.

– António, não contes a ninguém, mas estou com muitas saudades de casa... principalmente da minha mãe!

– Eu sei eu percebo. Foi hoje o dia em que ela...? – perguntou António.

– Não, mas era hoje o **aniversário** dela. É impossível não ficar um bocadinho triste a pensar nisso. Além disso, custa-me estar aqui a divertir-me, enquanto o meu irmão e o meu pai estão em casa a pensar nisto, sozinhos.

– Claro, é normal que te sintas assim, mas eles de certeza que estão bem e que acham bem tu estares aqui. Eu também tenho muitas saudades da minha irmã. Sei que não é a mesma coisa, mas... – respondeu António.

– Que se passa malta? Vá, venham para aqui! Desafio-vos a entrar no **canal**! Está **gelado**! E todos nus! – disse Tiago.

– Vamos Miguel, vai fazer-nos bem distrair-nos um bocadinho. E assim que entrarmos naquela água gelada, de certeza que não nos vamos conseguir lembrar de mais nada! – disse António.

– António, don't tell anyone, but I really miss home... especially my mother!

– I know, I understand. Was today the day she...? – asked António.

– No, but it was her birthday today. It's impossible not to get a little sad thinking about it. Besides, it upsets me that I'm here having fun, while my brother and father are at home thinking about it, by themselves.

– Sure, it's only natural that you feel that way, but for sure they are okay and think it's fine that you're here. I miss my sister a lot too. I know it's not the same thing, but... – replied António.

– What's up, guys? Come on, get over here! I dare you to dive into the canal! It's freezing! And fully naked! – said Tiago.

– Come on, Miguel, it's going to be good for us to distract ourselves a little bit. And once we get into that icy water, I'm sure we won't be able to think of anything else! – said António.

Miguel e António juntaram-se então ao resto do grupo, que já se despia para entrar no canal. Apenas Diogo não ia entrar. Além de estar absolutamente a congelar, tinha medo de que alguém os apanhasse. O canal onde os amigos queriam nadar era público, obviamente, mas ele duvidava que o que estavam a fazer era legal. Tiago garantiu que era porque o seu tio era polícia e ele sabia essas coisas, portanto Diogo acalmou-se um bocadinho.

Miguel and António then joined the rest of the group, who were already getting out of their clothes so they could enter the canal. Diogo was the only one that wasn't going in. Besides the water being absolutely freezing, he was afraid that someone would catch them doing it. The canal in which the friends wanted to swim was obviously public, but he doubted that what they were doing was legal. Tiago assured him that it was because his uncle was a policeman and he knew these things, so Diogo relaxed a bit.

– Cuidado, Tiago! Não entres de uma vez que ainda te pára o coração ou assim! – avisou Diogo.

– Ai Diogo, deixas de ser medricas! Pareces um bebé! Vá, entra lá também! – E Tiago saltou para a água. – A água está óptima! – disse Tiago, a tremer.

– Deve estar deve! Sabes que estás **roxo** certo? – insistiu Diogo.

– A água está gelada! Entrar devagar é um sofrimento! – disse Miguel.

– Salta para dentro de uma vez; é mais fácil! – ajudou Tiago.

– Não faças isso! António, tu não és maluco para entrar, pois não? – disse Diogo.

– Bem, queria só poder dizer que o fiz! – respondeu-lhe António.

– Bem, se não entras, pelo menos vê se há polícia a vir. – disse Tiago.

– Polícia? Mas não disseste que era tudo legal? – respondeu assustado Diogo.

– Disse? Ah, bem, mas não é; menti! – E Tiago começou a rir-se.

– Be careful, Tiago! Don't go in at once or else your heart might stop or something! – warned Diogo.

– Diogo, stop being a chicken! You're like a baby! Come on, get in too! – And Tiago jumped into the water. – The water is fine! – said Tiago, shaking.

– It sure should be! You know you're purple, right? – insisted Diogo.

– The water is freezing! Walking in slowly is really painful! – said Miguel.

– Just go in at once; it's easier! – helped Tiago.

– Don't do that! António, you're not crazy to go in, are you? – said Diogo.

– Well, I just want to say I did it! – António replied.

– Well, if you're not coming in, at least check for any cops that might be heading this way. – said Tiago.

– Cops? But didn't you say that it was legal? – replied Diogo, frightened.

– Did I say that? Oh, well, but it's not; I lied! – And Tiago began to laugh.

O resto do grupo juntou-se a Tiago a rir-se da cara de medo de Diogo. Muito provavelmente era mesmo ilegal o que eles estavam a fazer, mas se a polícia os visse, de certeza que não ia acontecer nada de muito grave. Ainda assim, os amigos, principalmente Tiago, gostavam de se meter com Diogo, que de todos era o que acreditava sempre nas suas **mentiras**. E assim, no meio de gargalhadas e brincadeiras, António e Miguel foram-se mesmo esquecendo das saudades que tinham de casa e da família.

The rest of the group started laughing as well, just from looking at Diogo's frightened face. It was very likely that what they were doing was illegal, but if the police saw them, it would certainly not be a serious offense. Still, the friends, especially Tiago, liked to tease Diogo, who was the one who always believed their lies. And so, amidst the laughter and playing around, António and Miguel were slowly forgetting about how much they missed home and their family.

Depois de vários pedidos desesperados de Diogo, o grupo foi saindo da água e secando-se com toalhas. Na verdade, mesmo que Diogo não estivesse a insistir com eles para saírem, não iriam aguentar muito mais—já que aquela água estava mesmo gelada. Mesmo a água das praias mais frias de Portugal não se assemelhava àquela temperatura. Entretanto, a fome começou a chateá-los. Decidiram ir então ir comer.

After Diogo's countless and desperate requests, the group came out of the water and dried up with towels. In truth, even if Diogo didn't insist on them leaving, they wouldn't be able to stand it for much longer—since that water was really freezing. Even the water from the coldest beaches of Portugal did not even get close to that temperature. Meanwhile, hunger began annoying them. They decided to go find somewhere to eat.

Pelas ruas de Bruges, enfeitadas com lindíssimas decorações de Natal, os amigos andavam à procura do bar ideal para passarem a tarde—para beberem uns copos e comerem uns petiscos. Era Tiago que mostrava o caminho—já que era o único a conhecer aquelas ruas. Embora não tivesse dito ao resto do grupo, estava a dirigir-se exactamente para o café onde tinha conhecido a sua primeira namorada, uns anos antes, quando foi a Bruges numas férias de Natal com os pais.

Through the streets of Bruges, adorned with beautiful Christmas decorations, the friends were looking for the ideal bar to spend the afternoon—to have a few drinks and eat some snacks. It was Tiago who showed the way—since he was the only one to know those streets. Although he hadn't told a thing to the rest of the group, he was heading to the cafe where he had met his first girlfriend, a few years earlier, when he went to Bruges on a Christmas vacation with his parents.

Quando chegaram ao café que Tiago disse ser o melhor de Bruges para os convencer a escolher aquele, decidiram comer lá dentro já que fora estava muito frio. No entanto, e como estava um dia de sol, a **esplanada** estava cheia de pessoas. Estavam esfomeados, por isso chamaram logo o empregado de mesa. Cada um pediu um bife, mal passado, com batatas fritas, arroz, e um ovo estrelado. Para beber, pediram água e cerveja.

When they arrived at the cafe that Tiago said was the best in Bruges, to convince them to choose that one, they decided to eat inside since it was very cold outside. However, and as it was a sunny day, the space outside was full of people. They were starving, so they called the waiter immediately. Each ordered a steak, rare, with fries, rice, and a sunny side up egg. To drink, they asked for water and beer.

Enquanto esperavam pela comida, o grupo de amigos cedeu todo à nostalgia. Afinal, não era só António e Miguel que estavam com saudades de casa e da família. Diogo começou por dizer que estava a adorar estar com eles, e queria continuar, mas que já sentia falta dos avós, que era com quem ele vivia. Tiago dizia sempre que achava que era por isso que Diogo era tão mimado.

While they were waiting for the food, the group of friends gave in to nostalgia. After all, it wasn't just António and Miguel who missed their home and their family. Diogo started by saying that he was loving being with them, and wanted to keep at it, but that he missed his grandparents, which was who he lived with. Tiago would always say he thought that was why Diogo was so spoiled.

Tiago também não resistiu em falar dos seus sentimentos. Acabou por confessar que os tinha levado ali por causa do seu primeiro amor—Alice—, com esperança de que ela por algum motivo, estivesse no café quando eles lá fossem. Todos se riram mas entenderam.

Tiago couldn't resist talking about his feelings as well. He eventually confessed that he had taken them there because of his first love—Alice—, in hopes that she, for some reason, was in the cafe when they got there. They all laughed but understood.

– És um romântico profissional! – disse-lhe Diogo.

– Por falar em profissional, já és enfermeiro oficialmente ou não Diogo? – perguntou Miguel.

– Ainda não... Era suposto acabar este ano, mas falta-se uma cadeira...

– Bem, há quantos anos estás na faculdade, Diogo? Só os teus avós para aturar isso, realmente! – disse António.

– Aos mesmos anos que o aqui Sr. Arquitecto Tiago... – respondeu Diogo.

– Ou seja, há muitos! – brincou Miguel.

– Goza goza, oh Sr. Doutor, cheio de sucesso! O que eu devia ter sido era escritor, ou cantor, ou poeta, ou pintor, ou actor... Algo ligado à arte, onde eu pudesse expressar a minha veia romântica! – respondeu Tiago, com um sorriso.

– Pois, ias ter jeito! – disse António. – Eu gostava era de ter sido jogador de futebol!

– Não te preocupes; que és melhor fisioterapeuta que jogador de bola! – brincou Tiago, e todos se riram.

– You're a professional romantic! – said Diogo.

– Speaking of professional, are you a nurse officially or not, Diogo? – asked Miguel.

– Not yet... It was supposed to end this year, but I still have one class left...

– Well, for how many years have you been in college, Diogo? Only your grandparents to put up with it, really! – said António.

– The same amount years as Mr. Architect Tiago here... – replied Diogo.

– So, that means a lot of years! – joked Miguel.

– Laugh all you want, you successful Mr. Doctor! What I should have been was a writer, or singer, or poet, or painter, or actor...

Something that had to do with art, where I could express my romantic spirit! – replied Tiago, with a smile.

– Yes, you'd be good doing that! – said António. – I would have liked to be a football player!

– Don't fret about it; you're a better physiotherapist than football player! – joked Tiago, and everyone laughed.

Apesar de se estarem a divertir, Miguel tinha voltado a pensar na mãe. Estava a divertir-se, mas não conseguia **afastar** a tristeza. Entretanto, a comida veio, e os amigos quase não falavam. Nem repararam que na mesa ao lado estava uma família portuguesa, a falar muito alto. Uma menina dessa família tinha um chapéu de **aniversariante**. Dali a uns minutos, o empregado de mesa veio com o bolo de aniversário, e a família começou a cantar os parabéns:

Although they were having fun, Miguel had gone back to thinking about his mother. He was having fun, but he couldn't keep the sadness away. Meanwhile, the food came, and the friends hardly spoke. They didn't even notice that, on the next table, there was a Portuguese family, talking very loudly. A girl from this family had a birthday hat. In a few minutes, the waiter came with the birthday cake, and the family began to sing "Happy birthday":

"Parabéns a você, nesta data querida, muitas felicidades, muitos anos de vida. Hoje é dia de festa, cantam as nossas almas. Para a menina Marta, uma salva de palmas!"

"Happy birthday to you, happy birthday to you, happy birthday dear Marta, happy birthday to you!"[19]

Ao ouvir isto, Miguel começou a chorar—era o aniversário da sua mãe, e o nome dela era Marta. Uma senhora da família portuguesa da mesa ao lado reparou em Miguel emocionado, e por preocupação,

---

[19] The "Happy Birthday" song is different in both languages—the English version isn't a literal translation of the Portuguese one.

perguntou discretamente a António o que se passava com o amigo. Quando a senhora percebeu tudo, disse logo:

When he heard this, Miguel began to cry—it was his mother's birthday, and her name was Marta. A lady from the Portuguese family from the next table noticed the emotional Miguel, and concerned for him, asked António, discreetly, what was happening to his friend. When the lady realized everything, she said:

– Há sempre lugar para mais um… Ou para mais quatro! Juntem-se a nós caros amigos!

– There is always room for one more... Or four more! Join us, dear friends!

E deu um forte abraço ao Miguel. Aquele **calor** tão português, e tão maternal, deixou Miguel de coração quente.

And she gave Miguel a big hug. That tenderness, so Portuguese and so maternal, left Miguel with a warm heart.

Sumário

Um grupo de amigos que está a viajar pela Europa num interrail há vários meses chega Bruges na Bélgica. Os amigos, António, Miguel,

Tiago e Diogo, começam a sentir falta de casa. Cada um sente também saudades dos seus entes queridos, mas divertem-se tanto que acabam por se distrair. Miguel, no entanto, está particularmente triste porque esse seria o dia de aniversário da sua mãe, que já tinha falecido. Enquanto estavam num café a comer e a conversar, algo inesperado mas banal aconteceu. É esse acontecimento que acaba por animar Miguel para o resto do dia.

Summary

A group of friends that are traveling across Europe in an interrail for several months arrives in Bruges in Belgium. The friends, António, Miguel, Tiago, and Diogo, start missing home. Each one also misses their loved ones, but they are having so much fun that they end up not thinking about it. Miguel, however, is particularly sad because that day would be his mother's birthday, and she had already passed away. While they were at a coffee shop eating and talking, something unexpected but ordinary happened. It was that event that ends up being what cheers Miguel up for the rest of the day.

Vocabulary List

Afastar – move away, remove, push away;

Ambiente – environment, climate;

Aniversariante – birthday boy/girl;

Aniversário – birthday;

Calor – heat, hot, but it in this context, it is used as meaning "warmth";

Canal – in the text used as canal, but it can also mean "channel", "conduit", "pipeline";

Comovido – moved, touched, emotional;

Esplanada – the outside tables at restaurants or bars;

Gelado – it means "ice cream" as a noun, "freezing" or "icy" as an adjective;

Luzes – lights;

Mentiras – lies;

Mês – month;

Natal – Christmas;

Roxo – purple;

Semana – week;

Suspiro – sigh, gasp.

Perguntas

1. O que está a fazer o grupo de amigos em Bruges?
2. Porque é que Miguel está triste?
3. Tiago convida-os para fazer qualquer coisa aventureira. O que é?
4. Porque os tinha levado Tiago àquele café em específico?

5. O que fez Miguel sentir-se melhor?

Escolha Múltipla

1. Em que altura do ano se passa a história?
   a) Primeira semana do mês de Dezembro;
   b) Primeira semana do mês de Janeiro;
   c) Segunda semana do mês de Dezembro;
   d) Primeira semana do mês de Novembro.
2. Quem, do grupo de amigos, não entra no canal?
   a) Tiago;
   b) António;
   c) Diogo;
   d) Miguel.
3. Porque estava roxo Tiago?
   a) Porque se pintou;
   b) Não estava—Diogo estava a mentir;
   c) Porque a água estava gelada;
   d) Porque tinha olheiras.
4. Que profissão Tiago acha que devia ter seguido?
   a) Polícia;
   b) Professor;
   c) Enfermeiro;
   d) Qualquer coisa ligada com a arte, para expressar os seus sentimentos e emoções.
5. Porque quase não falavam os amigos quando a comida veio?
   a) Porque se tinham chateado uns com os outros;
   b) Porque não lhes apetecia;
   c) Porque estava muito barulho e não se ouvia nada;
   d) Porque estavam cheios de fome e nem paravam para falar.

Questions

1. What is the group of friends doing in Bruges?
2. Why is Miguel sad?
3. Tiago invites them to do something adventurous. What is it?

4. Why did Tiago take them to that specific cafe?
5. What made Miguel feel better?

Multiple Choice

1. At what time of the year is the story happening?
   a) First week of December;
   b) First week of January;
   c) Second week of December;
   d) First week of November.

2. Who in the group of friends doesn't go in the canal?
   a) Tiago;
   b) António;
   c) Diogo;
   d) Miguel.
3. Why was Tiago purple?
   a) Because he painted himself;
   b) He wasn't—Diogo was lying;
   c) Because the water was freezing;
   d) Because he had dark circles under his eyes.
4. What profession does Tiago think he should have followed?
   a) Policeman;
   b) Professor;
   c) Nurse;
   d) Anything related to the arts, where he could express his feelings and emotions.
5. Why didn't the friends talk when the food got to the table?
   a) Because they were upset with each other;
   b) Because they didn't feel like it;
   c) Because it was very noisy and they couldn't hear anything;
   d) Because they were starving and didn't even stop to talk.

Respostas

1. Está a viajar pela Europa num InterRail.

2. Porque tem saudades da família, em particular, da mãe que já morreu.
3. Ele convida-os a saltar e nada no canal.
4. Porque foi lá que conheceu o seu primeiro amor, e tinha esperança de que ela lá estivesse.
5. O abraço da mulher que era da família Portuguesa que estava no café também.

Escolha Múltipla

1. a)
2. b)
3. c)
4. d)
5. d)

Answers

1. They were traveling across Europe in an InterRail.
2. Because he misses his family, especially his mother, who had passed away.
3. He invites them to dive and swim at Bruges' canal.
4. Because it was there that he met his first love, and hoped she might be there that day.
5. The hug from the woman from the Portuguese family that was there as well.

Multiple Choice

1. a)
2. b)
3. c)
4. d)
5. d)

Chapter 10 – O Novo Aluno

Maria, a professora, não estava a conseguir manter a ordem na sala de aula. Os alunos estavam muito **exaltados**, todos a falar por cima uns dos outros. O barulho que as suas vozes faziam ouvia-se a uma distância bastante considerável. Alguns professores passavam pela janela da sala de aula para ver o que se passava. Paravam e **espreitavam**, curiosamente, por uns segundos. A professora Maria acenava de dentro indicando que estava tudo bem, tudo controlado. Ainda assim, via os professores falando entre si do lado de fora, de testa franzida e cara preocupada. Assim se **mantinham** durante alguns segundos, e depois iam-se embora. Maria, a professora, não tinha **dúvidas** que embora eles tivessem partido, continuavam a comentar o sucedido à medida que iam caminhando.

Maria, the teacher, was unable to maintain order in the classroom. The students were very excited, talking over each other. The noise their voices made could be heard at a quite considerable distance. Some teachers were passing by the classroom window to see what was going on. They would stop and have a look, curiously, for a few seconds. Maria, the teacher, would wave from the inside, indicating that everything was well, everything was under control. Still, she would see the teachers talking outside, with a frown and a worried face. They would stay like that for a few seconds, and then they would leave. Maria, the teacher, had no doubt that even though they left, they would still be commenting on what happened as they were walking away.

Maria, a professora, sentia-se mal com os outros professores achavam dela. Maria era a mais velha professora naquela escola e também era a que tinha mais anos de experiência—quarenta e três. No entanto, por não ser nada autoritária, por usar métodos de ensino considerados **ultrapassados** e, principalmente, por não impor a sua vontade quando a **contrariavam**, os **colegas** mais novos não eram muito simpáticos para ela. Frequentemente gozavam com ela por trás das suas costas, e pela sua frente usavam bastante sarcasmo e cinismo, **desvalorizando** constantemente as suas opiniões. Maria, embora nada dissesse, ficava bastante afectada com tudo isto. Deixava-a triste saber que nenhum dos colegas a respeitava e que nunca ouviam, ou valorizavam o que ela dizia. Muitas vezes chegava a casa ao final do dia, onde morava com os seus dois gatos, e prometia a si mesma que no dia seguinte ia ser diferente. Que no dia, seguinte iria **bater o pé,** e fazer a sua voz ser ouvida. Mas de todas as vezes, todos os dias seguintes, nunca conseguiu arranjar a **coragem** para o fazer. Ao final da tarde, ao voltar para casa, depois das tentativas falhadas, sentia-se ainda pior—não só a tratavam mal, como ela permitia, e não tinha coragem para pôr fim a isso.

Maria, the teacher, felt bad about what the other teachers thought of her. Maria was the oldest teacher in that school, and also the one that had more years of experience—forty-three. Nevertheless, because she wasn't authoritarian, because she used teaching methods that were considered outdated and, especially, because she did not impose her will when someone went against it, her colleagues were not very nice to her. They would frequently make fun of her behind her back, and in front of her, they would use a lot of sarcasm and irony, minimizing constantly her opinions. Maria, even though she wouldn't say anything, was really upset about it. Knowing that no colleague respected, listened, or valued what she had to say made her sad. Many times, at the end of the day, she would get home, where she lived with her two cats, and would promise that the next day would be different. That the next day, she would put her foot down, and her voice would be heard. But every time, every next day, she was never able to find the courage to do it. At the end of the afternoon, when returning home, after the unsuccessful tries, she would feel even worse—not only would other people treat her badly, but she would also allow it, and didn't have the guts to stop it.

Além disto, também os alunos não lhe davam descanso. A sua personalidade impedia com que ela fosse **assertiva**. Para mais, as idades dos alunos com que ela lidava, eram propícias a um **comportamento irrequieto**. Além disso, o facto de virem de **bairros** mais **desfavorecidos**, onde viam no seu dia-a-dia coisas que as crianças não deveriam ver, definitivamente não ajudava. A grande maioria era bastante **mal-educada**, não respeitava ninguém, e não estava habituada a qualquer tipo de regras ou disciplina. Para alguém que fosse assertivo, controlar esta turma iria ser **complicado**; para alguém como professora Maria, quase impossível. Agora, tantos anos depois, a professora Maria já tinha deixado de tentar. Estava **deprimida**, frustrada, e sem **forças** para **inverter** o curso das coisas. Já não se importava com as consequências que o seu mau

desempenho poderia ter nem com o que os seus colegas diziam, nem com controlar os alunos tão malcomportados. Resumindo, já não se importava, ou isso dizia a ela própria, que a vida corresse como corria. O que importava, pensava ela, era que passasse rápido.

Besides this, the students wouldn't give her a rest as well. Her personality prevented her from being assertive. Furthermore, the age of the students she was dealing with was already a favorable factor to a restless behavior. Moreover, the fact that most of them came from poor neighborhoods, where they saw on a day-to-day basis things children shouldn't see, definitely didn't help. The great majority was really bad-mannered, didn't respect anyone, and wasn't used to following any type of rules or discipline. To someone that was assertive, controlling this class would be hard; to Maria, the teacher, it would be almost impossible. Now, so many years later, Maria, the teacher, had already stopped trying. She was depressed, frustrated, and without strength to change the course of things. She didn't mind anymore about the consequences her bad performance might bring or about what her colleagues said, or about controlling such ill-mannered kids. In sum, she didn't care, or at least that was what she told herself, that life was passing by as it was. What mattered, she thought, was that it went by fast.

A aula acabou, e os alunos saíram todos muito rapidamente, quase a **tropeçar** uns nos outros para serem os primeiros a chegar ao recreio. A indicação da aula ter acabado não tinha vindo da professora, nem dela tinha vindo a **autorização** para sair. O que tinha dado ordem de saída tinha sido a **campainha**, e ainda que a professora estivesse a falar, os alunos começavam a sair da sala de aula sem nunca olhar para trás, apesar dos inúmeros pedidos da professora para ficarem. No entanto, naquele dia havia algo diferente. Todos os alunos sairam, como normal. Todos, menos um. Maria, a professora, nem tinha reparado naquele aluno até o final da aula. Com todo o **tumulto** e confusão, não se tinha apercebido que existia uma cara nova. O novo aluno estava calmamente arrumar os seus **pertences** na sua mochila. À medida que arrumava duas canetas, uma vermelha e outra preta, e um lápis no estojo, a professora Maria olhava para o caderno aberto que ele tinha em cima da mesa. Espantada, levou a mão à boca, e por pouco não gritou. O que tinha visto deixou-a absolutamente surpreendida. O rapaz tinha feito **apontamentos** da aula. Este, ao arrumar o caderno, olhou, casualmente, para cima. Quando viu o choque da cara da professora Maria, ficou preocupado e perguntou:

The class was over, and the students left abruptly, almost tripping on each other to be the first to reach the playground. The indication that the class was over had not come from the teacher, nor from her originated the permission to leave the classroom. What gave them the order to leave was the bell, and even though the teacher was talking at that time, the students were abandoning the classroom without ever looking back, albeit the countless requests by the teacher asking them to stay. Nevertheless, that day, something was different. Every student had left, as normal. All but one. Maria, the teacher, hadn't even noticed that student until the end of the class. With all the commotion and chaos, she hadn't realized that there was a new face. The new student was calmly gathering his belongings into his backpack. While he was putting away two pens, one red and one black, and a pencil in a case, Maria, the teacher, was looking at the open notebook he had on the table. Astonished, she took her hand to her mouth to cover it, and she almost screamed. What she saw left her completely amazed. The boy had written some notes about the class. While he was packing his things, the student casually looked up. When he saw the face of shock the teacher had on her face, he got worried and asked:

– Sra. Professora, eeeestá tudo be... be... bem?

– Mrs. Teacher everything all... all... all right?

A professora Maria recuperou lentamente, e respondeu:

Maria, the teacher, recovered slowly, and answered:

– Sim, querido, está tudo bem. És novo aqui, não és?

– Siiim, Sra. Professora, cheguei à ci... ci... cidade a semana passaaaaada. – respondeu o aluno.

– Então e gostaste da aula? – perguntou a professora, com interesse na resposta.

– Sim. Não era muito fácil ouvir com o baru... baru... barulho todo, mas go... go... gosto muito da **matéria**. – disse o rapaz.

– Yes, dear, everything is all right. You're new here, aren't you?

– Yeees, Mrs. Teacher, I got here in this to... to... town laaaast week. – answered the student.

– And did you like the class? – asked the teacher, interested in the answer.

– Yes. It wasn't very easy to hear with all of the noi... noi... se, but I... I... I... I like the subject a lot. – said the boy.

A professora Maria não conseguia deixar de sentir uma ponta de vergonha com aquele brutal mas inocente comentário. E se antes estava **conformada** com como as coisas eram, agora sentia uma **sementinha** de força e esperança a **brotar**. O aluno e Maria continuaram numa longa conversa pela tarde fora, até que a professora reparou nas horas—eram então perto das 19h da tarde.

Maria, the teacher, couldn't help but feel a bit ashamed with that brutal but innocent comment. And if before she felt resigned with how things were, now she felt a little seed of strength and hope sprouting. The student and Maria kept talking all afternoon long, until the teacher noticed what time it was—close to 7 p.m.

– Uf! Estamos aqui na conversa desde as 16h da tarde. Talvez seja melhor ires andando para casa. Os teus pais devem estar a ficar preocupados. – disse a professora.

– Não, eles não vão se…se…sentir a miiiiiinha falta. – respondeu soturnamente o aluno.

– Uf! We have been here talking since 4 p.m. Maybe it's better that you go home. Your parents might be getting worried. – said the teacher.

– No, they wo… wo… won't miiiiss me. – answered the student sullenly.

O rapaz começou a contar a sua história à professora Maria. Ele tinha sido dado para adopção pelos seus pais, e vivia actualmente numa instituição. Tinha-se mudado para aquela cidade na semana passada porque a anterior instituição estava **sobrelotada**.

The boy then started telling his story to Maria, the teacher. He had been given up for adoption by his parents, and currently lived in an institution. He had moved to that town last week because the previous institution was overcrowded.

Os seus pais eram muito novos e quando o tinham tido, não estavam prontos para cuidar de uma criança. Todo o stress e ansiedade criados pelo mau-ambiente em casa, mais a passagem por várias instituições ao longo dos anos, criaram a **gaguez**, e o rapaz admitiu que se sentia muito **envergonhado** quando tinha que falar em público. O que acontecia era que os colegas gozavam com ele quando falava, e então ele calava-se. A professora Maria não conseguiu evitar que as lágrimas que estava a tentar esconder começassem a cair pelos seus olhos—é que os sentimentos que ele descrevia eram muito familiares. Só que a professora já há muito tempo que havia desistido de lutar por si. Até agora. Ver aquela criança, ainda tão nova, com tanta vida pela frente, e com o futuro cheio de potencial, fazia lembrar-se de si mesma. Prometeu não deixar que a mesma coisa acontecesse com ele. Por ele, e por causa dele, ganhou forças para lutar e prometeu que no dia seguinte, tudo iria ser diferente.

His parents were too young when they had him, and they weren't ready to take care of a child. All of the stress and anxiety created by the poor environment at home, plus living in several institutions over the years, created the stutter, and the boy admitted that he felt really embarrassed when he had to speak in public. What would happen was that his colleagues would make fun of him when he spoke, so he just shut up. Maria, the teacher, couldn't prevent the tears that she was trying to hide from falling from her eyes—the feelings that he was describing were much too familiar. But the teacher had long ago given up fighting for herself. Until now. Seeing that child, so young, with so much life ahead of him, with a future full of potential, reminded her of herself. She promised to not let the same thing happen to him. For him, and because of him, she gained strength to fight and promised that the next day, everything would be different.

E no dia seguinte assim foi. Quando chegou à sala, de aula não vinha cabisbaixa, mas com um sorriso confiante e determinado nos lábios. Os alunos já estavam na sala de aula, a fazer um barulho tremendo, como sempre. A professora Maria olhou para o novo aluno, que estava já escrever a data da lição no seu caderno e isso foi o empurrão que ela necessitava para fazer o que tinha decidido. Depois de respirar fundo uma vez, disse de forma sonora:

And the following day, that's what happened. When she arrived at the classroom, she wasn't feeling dejected, but with a determined and confident smile on her lips. The students were already in the classroom, making a fuss, as always. Maria, the teacher, looked at the new student, who was already writing the date of the lesson in his notebook, and that gave her the push she needed to do what she had decided. After a deep breath, she said loudly:

– Pouco barulho! Tudo calado, se faz favor!

– Be quiet! Everyone shut up, please!

O grito não tinha sido nada autoritário, e a voz tremeu até, mas os alunos calaram-se imediatamente—por ter sido algo tão inesperado—, e viraram-se para a professora. De seguida, disse então a professora Maria:

Her scream wasn't authoritarian at all, and her voice was even shaking, but the students shut up immediately—since it had been something so unexpected—, and they turned to the teacher. Following that, Maria, the teacher, said:

– Quero que se sentem nos vossos lugares, por favor. Obrigada. As coisas vão ser diferentes a partir de agora. Quem não gostar e não respeitar, tem bom remédio—vai directamente para o **gabinete** do director.

– I want you to sit down in your chairs, please. Thank you. Things will be different from now on. Whoever doesn't like it, has a good alternative—he or she can go straight to the principal's office.

Os alunos trocaram olhares entre eles. Alguns abanaram a cabeça, sem conseguir acreditar no que estava a acontecer, mas com medo de comprovar se o que a professora dizia era verdade ou não. Continuou então a professora Maria:

The students looked at one another. Some shook their heads in disbelief, but afraid to see if what the teacher was saying was true or not. Maria, the teacher, continued:

– Hoje vamos falar de uma matéria muito divertida. Tenha certeza de que vão gostar. Abram os vossos livros na página duzentos e trinta e sete, se faz favor.

– Today we're going to talk about a very fun subject. I'm sure you will like it. Open your books on page two hundred and thirty-seven, please.

E assim fizeram os alunos. O novo aluno não achou nada estranho ou diferente. Achou simplesmente que o dia anterior, o seu primeiro dia de aulas, tinha sido barulhento por mero acaso. Também não sabia que a história da sua vida, o seu interesse nas aulas, e a sua bondade tinham sido a causa deste novo ânimo da professora Maria. E antes de continuar a aula, a professora olhou pra ele e sorriu.

And the students did that. The new student didn't think any of it was strange or different. He simply thought that the previous day, the class was noisy by mere chance. He also didn't know that his life story, his interest in class, and his kindness were what caused Maria the teacher to gain this new spirit. And before she continued the class, the teacher looked at him and smiled.

Sumário

Maria, a professora, não conseguia manter a ordem na sua sala de aula. Já tinha muitos anos de experiência, mas a sua personalidade não a permitia ser assertiva. Por várias vezes tentou mudar, mas nunca conseguiu fazê-lo. Os seus colegas gozavam com ela, e os alunos não a respeitavam minimamente. Depois de um dia igual aos outros, reparou num novo aluno. Um aluno que, diferentemente dos outros, a respeitou. A conversa que teve com esse novo aluno fê-la ganhar força para mudar o rumo das coisas, e no dia seguinte as coisas foram mesmo diferentes.

Summary

Maria, the teacher, couldn't keep the order in her classroom. She had many years of experience, but her personality did not allow her to be assertive. For several times she tried to change, but she could never do it. Her colleagues made fun of her, and the students didn't respect her at all. After a day just like the others, she noticed a new student. A student who, unlike the others, respected her. The conversation she had with this new student made her gain strength to change the course of things, and the next day things were really different.

Vocabulary List

Apontamentos – notes;

Assertiva – assertive;

Autorização – authorization, permission;

Bairros – neighborhoods;

Bater o pé – being intransigent, literally: putting the foot down;

Brotar – sprout, bloom;

Campainha – bell, ring, doorbell;

Colegas – coworkers, colleagues;

Complicado – difficult, hard;

Comportamento – behavior;

Conformada – resigned, conformed;

Contrariavam – from the verb "contrariar" – "to oppose";

Coragem – courage, guts;

Deprimida – depressed, low;

Desempenho – performance;

Desfavorecidos – poor, underprivileged;

Desvalorizando – undermining, minimizing;

Dúvidas – doubt;

Envergonhado – ashamed, embarrassed;

Espreitavam – peeked;

Exaltados – excited, frantic, heated;

Gabinete – office;

Gaguez – stutter;

Inverter – reverse;

Irrequieto – restless;

Mal-educada – bad-mannered, rude;

Mantinham – maintained, kept, from the verb "manter" – "to keep";

Matéria – subject, but it can also mean "matter";

Pertences – belongings;

Sementinha – little seed, from "seed" – "semente";

Sobrelotada – overcrowded;

Tropeçar – trip over something or someone;

Tumulto – turmoil, riot, commotion;

Ultrapassados – outdated, overtaken, obsolete.

Perguntas

1. Porque não eram os colegas da professora Maria muito simpáticos com ela?
2. Como era maioria dos alunos?
3. O que houve de diferente naquele dia?
4. O que deixou a professora Maria um pouco envergonhada?
5. O que levou a professora a mudar a sua atitude?

Escolha Múltipla

1. Quem gozava Maria por detrás das suas costas?
   a) Os alunos;
   b) O novo aluno;
   c) O director da escola;
   d) Os seus colegas.
2. Onde vivia a grande maioria dos seus alunos?
   a) De bairros ricos;
   b) Do estrangeiro;

c) De bairros desfavorecidos;

d) Do centro da cidade.

3. O que punha o novo aluno no estojo?

   a) Dois lápis e duas canetas;

   b) Um lápis e duas canetas;

   c) Dois lápis e uma caneta;

   d) Um afia e uma borracha.

4. Onde vivia o novo aluno?

   a) Numa instituição;

   b) Num orfanato;

   c) Na casa dos pais;

   d) Na casa dos avós.

5. Que página mandou a professora abrir?

   a) 237;

   b) 337;

   c) 137;

   d) 37.

Questions

1. Why weren't Maria's colleagues very nice to her?
2. How was the majority of the students?
3. What was different that day?
4. What made Maria, the teacher, a bit embarrassed?
5. What led Maria, the teacher, to change her attitude?

Multiple Choice

1. Who mocked Maria behind her back?

   a) The students;

   b) The new student;

   c) The school's principal;

   d) Her colleagues.

2. Where did the great majority of her students live?

   a) In rich neighborhoods;

   b) Abroad;

c) In poor neighborhoods;
d) Downtown.

3. What was the new student putting in his case?
   a) Two pencils and two pens;
   b) One pencil and two pens;
   c) Two pencils and one pen;
   d) A sharpener and an eraser.
4. Where did the new student live?
   a) At an institution;
   b) At an orphanage;
   c) At his parents' house;
   d) At his grandparents' house.
5. What page of the book did the teacher say to open?
   a) 237;
   b) 337;
   c) 137;
   d) 37.

Respostas

1. Porque ela não era assertiva, os seus métodos de ensino eram considerados ultrapassados, e por causa da sua incapacidade para se impor.
2. A maioria dos alunos era irrequieta, mal-educada, e não respeitava nenhumas regras.
3. Um aluno ficou para trás, a arrumar calmamente os seus pertences. Tinha tirado apontamentos da aula.
4. O comentário inocente do rapaz sobre o quão barulhenta a aula tinha sido.
5. A história de vida do rapaz e o seu potencial para ter sucesso no future—ela não queria que ele se tornasse nela.

Escolha Múltipla

1. d)
2. c)
3. b)

4. a)

5. a)

Answers

1. Because she wasn't assertive, her teaching methods were considered old, and due to her inability to impose her will.
2. The majority of the students was restless, very bad-mannered, and didn't respect rules.
3. A student stayed behind, packing his belongings calmly. He had taken notes of the class.
4. The boy's innocent comment about how noisy the class was.
5. The boy's life story and his potential to be successful in the future—she didn't want him to become her.

Multiple Choice

1. d)
2. c)
3. b)
4. a)
5. a)

Chapter 11 – A Mentira Tem Perna Curta...

– Não há telemóveis à mesa! – disse a mãe de Tomás e Domingos. – Luís, ajuda-me! – acrescentou, virando-se para o **marido**.

– Vá, vá! – disse o pai, tomando o lado da mãe.

– No cellphones at the table! – said Tomás and Domingos' mother. – Luís, help me! – she added, turning to her husband.

– Come on, come on! – said the dad, taking the mom's side.

Tinha acabado de levantar os olhos do **jornal** que estava a ler, e se lhe perguntassem por que lhe estava a pedir ajuda a mulher, não saberia dizer; apenas repetia o que a mulher dizia.

He had just taken his eyes off of the newspaper that he was reading, and if somebody asked what his wife was asking, he wouldn't be able to tell; he just repeated what his wife said.

– Mas o Pai está a ler à mesa; é a mesma coisa! – protestou Tomás.

– Não podes ler isso mais tarde, Luís? – pediu a mãe.

– Ha? Ah! Sim, ok, desculpa. Isso! Façam o que vossa mãe vos pede. Já é a segunda vez que vos disse para lavar as mãos antes de comer, vá, vá! – disse o Pai.

– But Dad is reading at the table; it's the same thing! – protested Tomás.

– Can't you read that later, Luís? – asked the mom.

– Ha? Ah! Yes, okay, sorry. That's it! Do what your mother tells you to do. It is the second time I've told you to wash your hands before dinner, come on, come on! – said Dad.

Assim que ouviram isto, os três **puseram-se** a rir sem parar. O pai estava sempre muito distraído, e então quando estava **concentrado** a fazer outra coisa, como a ler o jornal, não conseguia mesmo tomar atenção a outra coisa. Assim que acabaram de comer, os irmãos, Tomás e Domingos, tiraram o telemóvel dos seus **bolsos**, sentaram-se no sofa, e começaram a **navegar** na internet. Estavam a passear pelo Instagram, Facebook, Twitter, como faziam não só todas as noites como grande parte do dia, todos os dias. A mãe já quase não conseguia ter uma conversa com os filhos, mas além disso ficava preocupada, pois não sabia no que eles andavam **metidos**. Ouvia as notícias dos perigos que a internet esconde, e queria estar a par de tudo para os poder proteger.

As soon as they heard this, the three started laughing without stopping. Dad was always very distracted, and when he was focused on doing something else, like reading the newspaper, he couldn't pay attention to anything else. When they finished eating, the brothers, Tomás and Domingos, took their phones out of their pockets, sat on the couch, and started surfing the internet. They were going through Instagram, Facebook, Twitter, something they did not only every night but most of the day, every day. Their mom almost couldn't have a conversation with them, but besides that, she was worried because she didn't know what they were up to. She kept hearing about the dangers that the internet hides, and she wanted to know everything so that she would be able to protect them.

– Domingos, o que é o Facebook? – perguntou a mãe, curiosa.

– É como se fosse um livro sobre ti, uma espécie de **diário** onde partilhas o quiseres, com quem quiseres. – respondeu o filho.

– Ai é? Mostras-me? – perguntou de seguida.

– Domingos, what is Facebook? – the mom asked, curious.

– It is like a book about you, a kind of diary where you share what you want, with whom you want. – the son answered.

– Is that right? Can you show me? – she then asked.

O filho **acedeu**, não sem antes fazer uma expressão de impaciência. Decidiu então mostrar à mãe o **mural** do seu Facebook, e algumas das **funcionalidades** que a aplicação tinha. A mãe ficou muito espantada. A ideia que tinha era outra. Era bom saber que se podia partilhar apenas com quem se queria e não com toda a gente. Então decidiu:

The son accepted, but not without making an expression of impatience. He decided to show his mother his Facebook wall, and some of the functionalities the app had. The mom was amazed. The idea she had about it was very different. It was good to know that he could share things only with who he wanted and not everybody. She then decided:

– Vou criar uma conta. Ajudas-me? – perguntou ao filho.

– O quê, Mãe? – gritou Tomás, levantando-se imediatamente do sofá.

– Qual é o problema? – respondeu a mãe.

– Nada, nada… – disse Tomás, **resignado**.

– I'm going to create an account. Will you help me? – she asked her son.

– What, Mom? – shouted Tomás, immediately getting up from the couch.

– What's the problem? – answered his mom.

– Nothing, nothing… – said Tomás, resigned.

Na verdade, tinha vergonha que a mãe visse as coisas que ele tinha no seu Facebook—não queria essa **intromissão** na sua vida. Não que tivesse alguma coisa de mal, mas afinal, era parte da sua privacidade em relação à Mãe. De seguida, a sua mãe, mostrando que tinha aprendido bem da explicação que o filho Domingos tinha feito, disse:

In truth, he was embarrassed that his mom would see the things he had on his Facebook—he didn't want that intrusion in his life. Not that there was anything wrong on his wall, but after all, it was a part of his privacy regarding his mom. After that, his mom, showing that she had learned well from the explanation Domingos gave her, said:

– Mas afinal não se mostra só a nossa página a quem se quiser?

– Sim, mas… – respondeu Tomás.

– Então, se não quiseres eu não preciso de ver o que tens na tua. Mas parece que tens alguma coisa a esconder! – disse ainda mãe.

– Não, Mãe, já está… – E continuou a **mexer** no telemóvel.

– But isn't it true that you only show the wall to who you want?

– Yes, but… – answered Tomás.

– So, if you want, I don't have to see what's on your wall. It just seems that you have something to hide! – said the mom.

– No, Mom, it's done… – And he kept playing with his phone.

Domingos ajudou então a mãe a criar uma conta. Depois mostrou-lhe com mandar pedidos de amizade. Naturalmente, enviou um pedido de amizade aos seus filhos, Tomás e Domingos. Luís não tinha uma conta. Meia hora depois, estava ela **entretida** no seu telemóvel, tal como os filhos, o pai que estava a ver televisão, **aproveitou** a **pausa** para anúncios e disse:

Domingos helped his mom create an account. After, he showed her how to send friend requests. Naturally, she sent a friend request to her sons, Tomás and Domingos. Luís did not have an account. Half an hour later, while she was playing with her phone, like her children, the dad who was watching television, used the break for commercials to say:

– Ena pá! Agora são tês viciados cá em casa! – E soltou uma gargalhada.

– Nem sequer compares as duas coisas, Luís! – respondeu a mãe.

– Ah pois é, Mãe. Agora já não nos podes dizer nada. Falta pouco para passares mais tempo ao telemóvel que nós, vais ver! – disse o Tomás, bem-disposto.

– Tomás olha lá, porque é que não aceitas o meu pedido de amizade? O Domingos já aceitou e alguns tios e primos teus também. O que tens tu a esconder afinal? No que é que andas metido? – perguntou a mãe, **curiosa,** mas também preocupada.

– Já vai, já vai. – respondeu Tomás, **frustrado**.

– Dang! Now we have three addicts in our house! – And laughed out loud.

– Don't even compare both things, Luís! – answered the mom.

– That's right, Mom. Now you can't say anything to us. In no time you'll be on your cell phone more than we are, you'll see! – said Tomás, in a good mood.

– Tomás, look, why don't you accept my friend request? Domingos accepted it already, and some of your uncles and cousins as well. What do you have to hide after all? What are you up to? – asked the mom, curious but also worried.

– I'm doing, I'm doing it. – answered Tomás, frustrated.

Não tinha nada a esconder, mas também não queria ter que pensar duas vezes antes de **postar** alguma coisa, sabendo que a mãe iria ver. No entanto, sentia não ter outra alternativa que não aceitar o pedido de amizade da mãe, portanto assim fez. A mãe começou logo a passear pelo mural do filho, vendo as fotos que este havia publicado, os comentários feitos, as músicas partilhadas, etc. No final, ficou aliviada. Como o filho tinha dito, não tinha nada a esconder.

He didn't have anything to hide, but he also didn't want to think twice before posting something, knowing his mom would see it. Nevertheless, he felt he didn't have any other choice than to accept the mother's friend request, so he did. His mom immediately started browsing through her son's Facebook wall, checking out the pictures he had published, the comments made, the shared music, etc. At the end of that, she was relieved. Like her son said, he had nothing to hide.

No dia seguinte de manhã ao pequeno-almoço, Tomás e Domingos já tinham saído de casa. "Já foram para a escola," pensou. Viu Luís, o marido, como sempre, a ler o jornal de manhã. Perguntou se tinha levado os miúdos, e porquê tão cedo.

The following day at breakfast, Tomás and Domingos were already gone from home. "They must be in school already," she thought. She saw Luís, her husband, as always, reading the morning newspaper. She asked if he had taken the kids, and why so early.

– Sim, sim. – respondeu Luís, **distraidamente**.

– Yes, yes. – answered Luís, impatiently.

"Alguma **reunião** de um **grupo de trabalho**", pensou a mãe. Na verdade, ela não sabia sequer porque tinha perguntado. O marido era sempre tão distraído que podia passar um dia inteiro sem ter **consciência** do que estava a fazer. A mãe começou então a preparar-se para o seu dia. Foi só bem depois das 18h, hora em que os seus filhos chegavam normalmente a casa, que a mãe começou a preocupar-se. Os filhos ainda não tinham chegado, e sempre que se **atrasavam** avisavam. Experimentou ligar aos dois. Nenhum atendeu. Deixou mensagens, esperando que nada tivesse acontecido. Perguntou ao marido se lhe tinham dito algo quando os tinha ido levar.

"Some group meeting," thought the mother. In truth, she didn't know why she had asked. The husband was always so distracted that a day could go by without having any awareness of what he was doing. The mom then started getting ready to face her day. It was only way after 6 p.m., time that her sons usually got home, that the mother started to get worried. The kids had not yet arrived, and they would always say something every time they were late. She tried calling both. Neither picked up. She left messages, hoping nothing bad had happened. Then, she asked her husband if they had told him something when he dropped them off.

– Não, não. Sabes como são os miúdos. – **balbuciou** Luís, desinteressadamente.

– No, no. You know how the kids are. – said Luís, uninterestedly.

Foi então que o seu telemóvel tocou. Era Domingos.

It was then that her phone rang. It was Domingos.

– Olá! – A sua voz parecia **tranquila**.

– Onde estão vocês? Está tudo bem? – perguntou, preocupada.

– Sim, Mãe, viemos para a casa do Fábio fazer um trabalho de grupo. Vamos demorar mais um pouco. Talvez tenhamos que ficar cá em casa a dormir. Tu sabes, para aproveitar o tempo ao máximo para trabalhar. – respondeu Domingos.

– Ah! Deixaram-me tão preocupada! Mas então vão ficar a trabalhar durante fim-de-semana, é? Querem que vos vá buscar amanhã? – perguntou a Mãe, aliviada.

– Não, Mãe! – respondeu Domingos, muita **apressadamente**. – Quando acabarmos o pai do Fábio leva-nos a casa. Não te preocupes. – E desligou.

– Hi! – His voice sounded calm.

– Where are you? Is everything all right? – she asked, worried.

– Yes, Mom, we came over to Fábio's to work on an assignment for school. We are going to take a while longer. Maybe we'll have to stay here for the night. You know, make the most out of it. – answered Domingos.

– Ah! You guys left me so worried! But are you going to stay there during the weekend? You want me to pick you up tomorrow? – asked Mom, relieved.

– No, Mom! – answered Domingos, very quickly. – When we're done, Fábio's dad will take us home. Don't worry. – And he hung up.

Mais calma, a mãe ficou, no entanto, com **a pulga atrás da orelha**. Para se distrair, pegou no telemóvel. Depois de uns minutos pelo Facebook, viu uma foto nova no perfil Tomás. Estava com um **sorriso de orelha a orelha**. No entanto, algo parecia estranho. Algo estava mal na fotografia. Foi então que reparou na Torre dos Clérigos atrás de Tomás! Estava a olhar para a fotografia e Tomás estava **vestido** com uma T-shirt que tinha recebido no seu aniversário, um mês antes. E desde então ainda não tinham ido ao Porto. A mãe não estava a acreditar no que estava a ver. Foi imediatamente contar o que tinha descoberto ao marido. Luís pareceu surpreendido, como sempre.

Calmer, however, the mother sensed that something wasn't quite right. To distract herself, she picked up her phone. A few minutes after surfing Facebook, she saw a new picture in Tomás' profile. He had a smile from ear to ear. Something seemed off, however. Something about the picture was wrong. It was then that she noticed the Clérigos' Tower behind Tomás! She was looking at the picture and also saw that Tomás was wearing a T-shirt he had received for his birthday, a month before. And since then, they hadn't been to Oporto. The mother couldn't believe what she was seeing. She immediately went to her husband to tell him about what she had found out. Luís seemed surprised, as always.

– Os miúdos estão no Porto?

– O Tomás pelo menos está. Mas muito provavelmente o Domingos também! – disse-lhe a mulher.

– Olha que estranho! – respondeu Luís.

– De certeza que eles não te disseram nada quando os foste levar à escola? Pensa lá bem! – insistiu a mulher.

– À escola? Não, eu deixei-os no aeroporto! – respondeu o marido.

– No aeroporto? Estás louco? E não estranhaste os miúdos irem para o aeroporto num dia as aulas?! – disse, muito **irada**.

– The kids are in Oporto?

– Tomás, at least, is. But it is very likely that Domingos is as well! – said the wife.

– That's weird! – answered Luís.

– Are you sure that they didn't tell you anything when you dropped them off at school? Think about it! – the wife insisted.

– At school? No, I dropped them off at the airport! – answered the husband.

– At the airport? Are you crazy? And you didn't think it was strange that they would go to the airport on a school day?! – she said, very angrily.

Ligou para os filhos e disse que já sabia de tudo. Domingos pediu desculpas e prometeu voltar ainda essa noite. O pai riu-se assim que percebeu tudo que tinha acontecido, o que por sua vez deixou a mulher mais relaxada. Foi então que Luís disse:

She then called her sons and told them she knew about everything. Domingos apologized and promised to return that very same night. Dad laughed as soon as he realized what had happened, which in turn left the wife a bit more relaxed. It was then that Luís said:

– Oh, deixa lá. Eles estão bem. Foram só divertir-se. Não te lembras de quando nós fomos passar um fim-de-semana ao **Alentejo**? Tínhamos a idade deles e também ninguém sabia! Além disso, pode servir de uma boa lição: mais rápido se apanha um mentiroso que um coxo!

– Oh, just leave it. They're okay. They just went to have fun. Don't you remember when we went to spend the weekend in Alentejo? We were their age, and nobody knew as well! Besides, it can become a good lesson for them: a person that lies is caught faster than a person who limps![20]

A mãe, preocupada com os filhos e **chateada** por eles lhe terem mentido, sorriu poque sabia que o marido tinha razão.

The mom, worried about the kids and upset because they lied to her, smiled because she knew her husband was right.

Sumário

---

[20] This sentence is a literal translation of the famous proverb that is written in the Portuguese version.

Tomás e Domingos são os típicos jovens—sempre com o telemóvel na mão a navegar na internet, principalmente nas redes sociais. O pai é muito distraído e nunca liga a nada, enquanto a mãe insiste para que eles, pelo menos, à mesa deixem os telemóveis no bolso. Além disso, fica preocupada com os perigos que a internet esconde. No entanto, fica intrigada acerca do que são as redes sociais e percebe que não é assim tão mau. Na verdade, acaba por ser o Facebook que a ajuda a desvendar um grande mistério...

Summary

Tomás and Domingos are typical young boys—always with their mobile phones in their hands, surfing the internet, especially surfing their social networks. Their father is always absent-minded and never pays attention to anything, while the mother insists that they, at least, leave the phones in their pockets when they are at the dinner table. Moreover, she is concerned with the dangers that the internet hides. However, she is puzzled about what social networks are and realizes that it is not so bad after all. In fact, Facebook turns out to be what helps her uncover a great mystery...

Vocabulary List

A pulga atrás da orelha – literally: "a flea behind the ear". It means being suspicious of something;

Alentejo – a Portuguese region between Lisbon and Algarve;

Apressadamente – quickly, hurriedly;

Aproveitou – took advantage of, enjoyed, seized;

Balbuciou – babbled, stammered:

Bolsos – pockets;

Concentrado – focused, centered, concentrated:

Curiosa – curious, interested, intriguing;

Diário – diary, but also "daily";

Entretida – entertained, amused;

Frustrado – frustrated, thwarted;

Funcionalidades – functionalities, functions, features;

Intromissão – intrusion, interference, meddling;

Irada – angry, irate, enraged;

Jornal – newspaper;

Marido – husband;

Metidos – literally: when something is kept inside something else, but in this context, it refers to someone who is up to something;

Mexer – to touch something with your hands, to move, to stir;

Mural – in this context, the Facebook wall, but also means "mural"

Navegar – used like "surfing" in the internet context, but literally it means "to navigate";

Pausa – in this context, the break for commercials, but it literally means "pause";

Postar – word adapted from the English verb "to post", used in the social network context. The correct Portuguese word to use would be "publicar" – "to publish";

Sorriso de orelha a orelha – literally: smile from ear to ear;

Tranquila – relaxed, laidback;

Vestido – as a noun it means "dress", as an adjective "dressed", from the verb "to dress" – "vestir".

Perguntas

1. Porque queria a mãe criar uma conta de Facebook?
2. Tomás não queria que a mãe tivesse uma conta. Porquê?
3. O que pensou a mãe quando não viu os filhos ao pequeno-almoço?
4. Onde estavam os filhos, afinal?
5. Como descobriu a mãe onde eles estavam?

Escolha Múltipla

1. Luís estava a ler o quê à mesa?
   a) Uma revista;
   b) O jornal;
   c) Um livro;
   d) Um folheto.
2. O marido era muito…?
   a) Atento;
   b) Rabugento;
   c) Distraído;
   d) Emotivo.
3. A que horas começou a preocupar-se a mãe por os filhos não estarem em casa?
   a) Às 18h;
   a) Bem depois das 18h;

b) Antes das 18h;

c) Pouco depois das 18h.

4. Que peça de roupa ajudou a mãe a descobrir que a foto de Tomás não era antiga?

a) Um casaco;

b) Os sapatos;

c) Uma T-shirt;

d) As calças.

5. O que tinham ido visitar os pais quando tinham a idade dos filhos?

a) Porto;

b) Alentejo;

c) Aeroporto;

d) Torre dos Clérigos.

Questions

1. Why did the mother want to create a Facebook account?
2. Tomás didn't want his mother to have an account. Why?
3. What did the mother think when she didn't see her sons at breakfast?
4. Where were they after all?
5. How did the mother find out where they were?

Multiple Choice

1. What was Luís reading at the table?

a) A magazine;

b) The newspaper;

c) A book;

d) A leaflet

2. Luís was very…?

a) Focused;

b) Cranky;

c) Absent-minded;

d) Emotional.

3. At what time did the mother start worrying that their kids weren't home?
   a) At 6 p.m.;
   b) Well after 6 p.m.;
   c) Before 6 p.m.;
   d) A bit after 6 p.m.
4. What piece of clothing helped the mother figure out Tomás' picture wasn't an old one?
   a) A coat;
   b) The shoes;
   c) A T-shirt;
   d) The pants.
5. What did the parents visit when they were their sons age?
   a) Oporto;
   b) Alentejo;
   a) Airport;
   b) Clérigos' Tower.

Respostas

1. Porque queria ver o que os filhos andavam a fazer.
2. Porque não queria a mãe a intrometer-se na vida dele.
3. Que já tinham ido para a escola.
4. No Porto.
5. Por uma fotografia que viu de Tomás no Facebook.

Escolha Múltipla

1. b)
2. c)
3. b)
4. c)
5. b)

Answers

1. Because she wanted to see what her kids were up to.
2. Because he didn't want his mother meddling in his life.
3. That they had gone to school already.
4. Oporto.
5. Through a picture Tomás posted on Facebook.

Multiple Choice

1. b)
2. c)
3. b)
4. c)
5. b)

False cognates

Now that you have reached the end of the book, here are some common mistakes that usually arise when encountering words that are known as "false friends". These have been compiled so that you can access this list at any given moment to easily recognize them and avoid mistakes in the future.

However, there are also very simple translations. There are a few strategies[21] you can follow many times to get the word you are looking for in Portuguese easily. For instance, the English suffix "*ty*" is equivalent to the Portuguese suffix "*dade*". So, you just need to switch one for the other, while the rest of the word stays the same:

❖ Calami-*ty* = Calami + *dade* ➡ Calami*dade*
❖ Sani*ty* ➡ Sani*dade*
❖ Vani*ty* ➡ Vani*dade*
❖ Prosperi*ty* ➡ Prosperi*dade*

---

21 Bear in mind that there are several exceptions to these rules and that you should always check the correct meaning of the word in the dictionary, as well as the context it is used in, before trying to use it yourself.

The English suffix *"tion"* is equivalent to the Portuguese suffix "*ção*". The method is the same:

- ❖ Formaliza*tion* = Formaliza + *ção* ➡ Formaliza*ção*
- ❖ Lo*tion* ➡ Lo*ção*
- ❖ Constipa*tion* ➡ Constipa*ção*
- ❖ Emigra*tion* ➡ Emigra*ção*

For the adverbs of manner, which usually end in *"ly"*, you just have to switch it for *"mente"*:

- ❖ Oficial-*ly* = Oficial + *mente* ➡ Oficial*mente*
- ❖ *Orally* ➡ Oral*mente*
- ❖ Forma*lly* ➡ Formal*mente*
- ❖ Similar*ly* ➡ Similar*mente*

Most words that end with *"ence"* in English, end with *"ência"* in Portuguese:

- ❖ Eloqu-*ence* = Eloqu + ência ➡ Ess*ência*
- ❖ Rever*ence* ➡ Rever*ência*

The same for words that end with *"ance"* in English—you just switch to *"ância"* in Portuguese:

- ❖ Eleg*ance* ➡ Eleg*ância*
- ❖ Ignor*ance* ➡ Ignor*ância*

Also, most of the words that end in *"ing"*, *i.e.*, verbs in the gerund or present participle form, end with *"ndo"*, even if the first part of the word is spelled differently. You do have to cut the last consonant, however. For instance:

- ❖ Eat – eat + ing ➡ Comer – come~~r~~ + ndo = come*ndo*
- ❖ Talk – talking ➡ Falar – fala~~r~~*ndo*
- ❖ Smile – smiling ➡ Sorrir – sorri~~r~~*ndo*

As for the misleading words, have a look at this small list of "false friends":

- ❖ Actualmente ➡ Currently ⇹ Actually ➡ Na verdade, na realidade
- ❖ Advertir ➡ to warn or advise ⇹ Advertise ➡ Publicitar

- ❖ Apontamento ➡ Note   Appointment ➡ Marcação
- ❖ Data ➡ Date 🔁 Data ➡ Dados
- ❖ Diversão ➡ Fun 🔁 Diversion ➡ Distracção, desvio
- ❖ Educado ➡ Polite 🔁 Educated ➡ Instruído, culto
- ❖ Esperto ➡ Smart 🔁 Expert ➡ Perito, especialista
- ❖ Esquisito ➡ Strange 🔁 Exquisite ➡ Belo, refinado
- ❖ Eventualmente ➡Possibly, maybe🔁   Eventually ➡ Finalmente, por fim
- ❖ Excitante ➡ Arousing 🔁 Exciting ➡ Empolgante
- ❖ Êxito ➡ Success 🔁 Exit ➡Saída
- ❖ Gripe ➡ Flu 🔁 Grip ➡ Agarrar
- ❖ Lanche ➡Midday snack 🔁 Lunch ➡Almoço
- ❖ Largo ➡ Broad, wide, or patio 🔁 Large ➡ Grande
- ❖ Legenda ➡ Subtitles 🔁 Legend ➡ Lenda
- ❖ Maior ➡ Bigger 🔁 Mayor ➡ Prefeito
- ❖ Parentes ➡ Relatives 🔁 Parents ➡ Pais
- ❖ Polícia ➡ Police 🔁 Policy ➡ Políticas
- ❖ Preservativo ➡ Condom 🔁 Preservative ➡ Conservante
- ❖ Puxar ➡ Pull 🔁 Push ➡ Empurrar
- ❖ Realizar ➡ Accomplish 🔁 Realize ➡ Perceber, dar-se conta
- ❖ Recordar ➡ To remember🔁 Record ➡ Gravação
- ❖ Resumir ➡ Summarize 🔁 Resume ➡ Recomeçar, retomar
- ❖ Taxa ➡ Fee 🔁 Tax ➡ Imposto
- ❖ Terrível ➡ Terrible 🔁 Terrific ➡ Excelente

Conclusion

A viagem chegou ao fim! Esperamos que tenha sido divertida![22]

Ideally, you should understand what was written! If not, don't give up—learning a language is hard, and Portuguese doesn't make it any easier. Once again, and as stated in the introduction chapter, the ultimate goal of the book was to instill in you an intuitive feel for the understanding of the language, so that you can "wield" it just enough to speak it when meeting Portuguese people, visiting a Portuguese-speaking country, or just trying it out with your friends for fun.

The method adopted—storytelling—was chosen to do just that. Stories are motivating and fun, engaging and interesting, and should help develop positive attitudes towards a foreign language. A story exercises the imagination, all while creating memory clues which the reader will, hopefully, connect. It's expected that, for example, the name of a random object comes to mind only by remembering a story that you read in this book. To continue with the example, the sight of that same thing—say a sandcastle—, will trigger the memory clue that will take you to Chapter 2. The images and illustrations can also have a role in achieving that purpose. Plus,

---

22 In case you need a bit of help: "The journey has come to an end! We hope it has been fun!"

there is the *personal involvement* effect. The relationship that is created with the characters and narrative helps at the moment your brain is creating a bridge between the story and the subjects it is teaching.

Moreover, if you want to teach all that you know to children or other curious and knowledge-thirsty adults yourself, this book can definitely help. It has been widely reported that the semi-communicative method (storytelling) has effective results, especially with children. So, it might be a great idea, with tremendous benefits for the teacher (you), to use the method of telling a story—literally. This way, the learner can learn while you're practicing your accent and pronunciation. Additionally, you will get the chance to be tested on the knowledge you think you already mastered, which is an infallible way to strengthen your knowledge on any given topic. The only thing you need to do to be the best Portuguese teacher you can is to adapt the content of the stories to the adequate level of difficulty. So, for instance, you might want to:

❖ Decide whether to keep or leave certain words, like unfamiliar or complicated words, idiomatic expressions, etc.;
❖ Simplify the grammar of a story, adapting verb tenses, or the structure of a phrase;
❖ Check the sentences' lengths and complexity, the way ideas are linked or explained, and so on.

Storytelling can, and we hope it did, create a desire to continue learning. So last, but not least—KEEP PRACTICING!

Printed in the USA
CPSIA information can be obtained
at www.ICGtesting.com
LVHW091928020624
782067LV00003B/320

9 781647 480219